3-D

D0129000

Functions of American English
Student's Book

Functions of American English

Communication activities for the classroom

Student's Book

Leo Jones
C. von Baeyer

The right of the
University of Cambridge
to print and publish
all kinds of books
was granted by law
in 1534.
The University has printed
and published continuously
since 1584.

Cambridge University Press
Cambridge
New York   New Rochelle
Melbourne   Sydney

Published by the Press Syndicate of the University of Cambridge
The Pitt Building, Trumpington Street, Cambridge CB2 1RP
32 East 57th Street, New York, NY 10022, USA
10 Stamford Road, Oakleigh, Melbourne 3166, Australia

© Cambridge University Press 1983

First published 1983
Sixth printing 1987

Printed in the United States of America

Library of Congress Cataloging in Publication Data
Jones, Leo, 1943–
Functions of American English

1. English language – Text-books for foreigners.
2. English language – Conversation and phrase books.
3. Americanisms.   I. von Baeyer, C.   II. Title.
PE1128.J6   1983   428.3'4   82-14716
ISBN 0 521 28528 3 (Student's Book)
ISBN 0 521 28529 1 (Teacher's Manual)
ISBN 0 521 24211 8 (Cassette)

Contents

Acknowledgments

Functions of American English is based on the British text *Functions of English* by Leo Jones, first published in 1977, then revised in 1981. Thanks to everyone who used and made such helpful comments on the British editions. In particular, thanks to Sue Gosling for her perceptive ideas and encouragement. And many thanks to all those who contributed to this American English adaptation, especially: Michael Sutton, who contributed his great cultural insight, generous encouragement, and much long, hard work; Adrian du Plessis, who made it all happen; Anna Fuerstenberg, without whom there would not be a fine recording; Ellen Shaw, Rhona Johnson, Sandra Graham, and Deborah Menzell who polished and presided over the final stages; and Edwinna von Baeyer, who helped at every stage and found many a lurking inconsistency.

The authors and publishers are grateful to the following for permission to reproduce illustrations and photographs: M.J. Quay (pages 4, 10, 15, 21, 26, 31, 38, 43, 48, 53, 60, 66, 72, 78, 84); Nilda Scherer (pages 7, 13, 18, 20, 24, 29, 33, 35, 40, 42, 47, 50, 62, 64, 68, 70, 79, 83, 89, 94, 108, 111, 124, 127, 131, 133, 144); Capitol Records (page 12); Tom Huffman (page 16); Columbia Pictures (page 25, first and second from left); courtesy 20th Century Fox (page 25, third from left); United Artists (page 25, fourth from left); Ted Draper (page 37); Mature Temps, Inc. New York City (page 58, left); Recreation Division, Dept. of Local Government, N.W.T. (page 58, right); Tandy Corporation (page 59); Miami Beach Visitor and Convention Authority (page 74); American Airlines (page 75, top left); N.Y. Convention and Visitors Bureau (page 75; top right); Washington Convention and Visitors Association (page 75; bottom left); Frederic Lewis, N.Y. (page 76); Universal Press Syndicate (page 80); United Features Syndicate, Inc. (pages 85, 86); Simpson-Sears, Ltd. (pages 92, 102, 118); Peter Kneebone (pages 100, 112, 116, 141, 142, 145); Romano Palace Hotel (page 129); Polaroid Corporation (page 138); Nassau Beach Hotel (page 146).

Cover design by Frederick Charles Ltd.
Cover photographs by David Groskind
Book design by Peter Ducker

Cassette production by C. von Baeyer and Anna Fuerstenberg; Speakers: Steven Bush, Sharon Corder, Anna Fuerstenberg, Sandi Ross, Leon Sobieski, Bruce Vavrina; Engineer: David Beare.

Introduction to the student

Please read this Introduction carefully to get to know the aims and methods of this book.

Who is this book for?

Functions of American English is for high intermediate and advanced learners who feel confident about using basic English grammar and vocabulary, and who are now ready to learn more about using English in real-life situations. This book is accompanied by a tape and a Teacher's Manual.

What does this book cover?

In order for your English to be effective, it must be appropriate to the situation you are in. So, when you are trying to choose the best way to express yourself in a particular situation, you have to keep in mind several things:
— What are you trying to do with your English sentences? Are you describing something, persuading someone, giving your opinion, or what? These are called *language functions*.
— What is your *role* in this situation? Are you a friend, stranger, employee, customer?
— Where are you talking? Is the *setting* on a plane, at a party, at a meeting?
— What are you talking about? Is the *topic* business, travel, sport?

Each unit in this book describes three important *language functions*. For example, the first unit covers "talking about yourself," "starting a conversation," and "making a date." The exercises in each unit let you practice all sorts of useful roles and topics in all sorts of typical places. You will practice the English that you know already and learn many useful new ways of saying things.

This book is just the starting point, though. There are many places in the book where you may want to ask your teacher for more information or for more time to practice some new material.

How is this book organized?

Each unit in *Functions of American English* is divided into several sections:

Conversation

This illustrates how each language function could be carried out during a conversation. Don't read the conversation section in the book until you have listened to the tape at least twice. This is *not* a "dialogue" that you have to learn by heart. Sometimes the teacher will tell you the situation that the conversation takes place in, and sometimes you should try to guess. The same six characters keep appearing in different situations throughout the book.

Presentations

The presentation sections include descriptions of the functions and various ways of carrying them out. When you come to a presentation, read it by yourself. Then keep your book closed while the teacher presents the ideas using the board and the tape, and asks you for your ideas. Make sure that you can pronounce the new expressions well. There are usually three presentations in a unit.

Exercises

There are several exercises after each presentation. The first one is often directed by the teacher, so that you have a chance to ask for help and advice. For the other exercises, the class is divided up into pairs or small groups of students who work on their own. Try hard to use new expressions that you have just learned in the presentation.

Many units have a Consolidation exercise at the end. In this kind of exercise you can practice expressions from all the presentations in the unit.

Communication activities

The exercises are often followed by instructions to look at a particular number in the *Communication activities* section at the back of this book. The activities involve two or more sides communicating with each other in discussions, role plays, problem-solving activities, etc. Each side has different instructions, printed on different pages so that the participants can't see each other's instructions. In this way you can have information that is different from your partner's information, just as in most real communication outside the classroom.

Please, don't prepare the communication activities ahead of time – let them be a surprise. And don't look at your partner's instructions – keep the activities spontaneous.

Try to experiment with different ways to get your point across in these activities. Be as talkative as you can – never just say *Yes* or *No*. And don't be afraid to make mistakes – learn from them! Your teacher will be going around from group to group to listen and help. At the end of each activity, the class will discuss difficulties, and the teacher will point out serious mistakes that would make a listener misunderstand something.

Written work

The written work at the end of each unit gives you further practice on some important items from the unit. Again, experiment with new ways of communicating.

The tape

▢ marks sections that are recorded on the cassette tape.

Conclusion

This book may be a little different from what you are used to. Don't be surprised – a course that teaches conversation must be a little unpredictable, since real-life conversations are so often unpredictable. We hope that you find working with these materials interesting and enjoyable.

1 Talking about yourself, starting a conversation, making a date

---

1.1 Conversation

John: Excuse me, is anybody sitting here?
Anne: Uh no . . . no, here, let me move my purse from the chair.
John: Oh, thank you. Say, haven't I seen you with Jack Davidson?
Anne: I work with Jack Davidson. How do you know Jack?
John: Oh, Jack and I went to school together. What sort of work do you do?
Anne: Oh, I . . . I work on commercial accounts at the trust company with Jack. Um . . . what do you do?
John: I'm a telephone installer – I just happen to be working on this street the last couple of days. I should introduce myself – my name's John Spencer.
Anne: Well pleased to meet you! I'm Anne Kennedy.
John: Happy to know you. Do you live around here?
Anne: Yeah, I live in the neighborhood – it's real convenient to work.
John: Oh, it sounds like . . .
[fade]
John: . . . Are you doing anything tonight?
Anne: Oh . . . uh, sorry, I'm afraid I'm busy tonight.

presentation

4

John: Well how about tomorrow? Maybe we could go to a movie.

Anne: Hey, that sounds like a great idea! Um ... do you like comedies?

John: Oh yeah, I like comedies ... uh, let's see, what could we see? How about *Bread and Chocolate*? I think that's playing over at ...

Anne: Ah ... .

John: ... on Main Street there.

Anne: That's a great idea.

John: Well I guess, uh, we should meet about eight o'clock then, 'cause I think the movie starts about eight-thirty. Uh, where would be a good place to meet?

Anne: There's ... uh ... there's a clock tower near the movie theater. We could meet there at about eight.

John: OK. That sounds good. See you tomorrow, then.

Anne: I'll see you then. Goodbye!

John: Bye-bye.

1.2 Presentation: talking about yourself

The presentation sections in this book usually give you some new expressions to learn. But for now, use the English you already know. The aim of the following three exercises is to give you a chance to get used to the methods that will be used throughout the book. Try to ask as many short questions as possible to get as much information as you can from your partner in each exercise. Try to answer in long sentences; keep talking; do not just say *Yes* or *No*. If you don't know what to say or how to continue, ask your teacher.

1.3 Exercise

Get together with another student. Introduce yourselves first and then find out about each other. Be friendly. Your teacher will demonstrate first. Here are some ideas to start off with, but ask for as much detail as possible. Ask about his or her:

FAMILY   Brothers and sisters. Parents. Childhood – happy? Home – where does he or she live?

FRIENDS   Many or just a few? What do they talk about and do together? Is it easy to make new friends?

EDUCATION   Different schools, colleges, or universities. Favorite subjects at school and why. Diplomas and degrees. Future plans.

EMPLOYMENT   Present job. What exactly does he or she do? Advantages and disadvantages. Previous jobs – details. Future plans.

FREE TIME   Hobbies. Sports. TV, radio, movies. What does he or she do on weekends and in the evening? What does he or she like to read?

TRAVEL   Countries visited. Parts of own country he or she knows. Languages. Favorite kind of vacation. Future plans.

After everyone has finished, tell the whole class the most interesting things you found out about your friend.

1.4   *Exercise*

Get together with a different student from the one you talked with in 1.3. Look at the questionnaire below. Help each other to fill in the blanks. Discuss how to answer the more difficult questions.

When you have finished, compare your answers with another pair of students. Give your completed questionnaire to your teacher to read and correct.

Questionnaire

Last name _____

First name _____

Nationality _____

Permanent address _____
_____

Present address _____
_____

Occupation or subject you are studying _____
_____

High school education _____
_____

Degrees or other qualifications _____

Other education and language courses _____
_____

What foreign languages do you speak and how well? _____
_____
_____

Have you ever lived in a place where people speak English most of the time? If so, for how long? _____
_____

What English textbooks have you used? _____
_____

When do you (or will you) need to use English? _____
_____
_____

In what areas does your English need the most improvement? _____
_____
_____

What is the main thing that you hope to get from this course? _____
_____
_____

1.5 *Exercise*

Imagine that you are at a cocktail party with the rest of the class. At a cocktail party everyone stands with a drink, chats for a few minutes to one guest, and then is expected to *circulate* and move on to another guest. The host or hostess (your teacher) normally speeds up the circulation by introducing guests to each other.
Now stand up and have a party! Talk to as many people as possible.

1.6 *Presentation: starting a conversation*

It is often difficult to make contact with strangers who speak another language – unless you know a few opening gambits, of course!
Here are some useful ways of starting a conversation with a stranger:

Nice day, isn't it?
Horrible weather we're having.
Excuse me, is anybody sitting here?
Say, don't I know you from somewhere?
Sorry, I couldn't help overhearing – did you mention something about …
Excuse me, have you got a light?
Uh, could you help me, I'm looking for …

Think of some situations where you would use each of these opening gambits. Decide with your teacher when they would be appropriate and what you might say next. Do people in your neighborhood start conversations with strangers in lineups, in stores, in buses?

1.7 *Communication activity*

To practice ways of starting a conversation, the class is divided into two groups: A and B. If you are in group A, look at communication activity 151 at the back of the book; if you are in group B, look at communication activity 38.

After you have made contact and had a short conversation, you may want to arrange another meeting. These are expressions you can use to arrange to meet someone:

Uh, are you going to be busy this evening?
Um, I was thinking of going to a movie tonight. Would you like to come?
Are you doing anything tonight? I was wondering if you'd like to go to a movie with me.
I'm going to a play with a group of friends. Would you like to join us?

YES! *That'd be very nice.*
       I'd love to.
       That's a great idea.

NO! *Sorry, I'm afraid I'm busy tonight.*
     Tonight's a problem. What about tomorrow night?
     Sorry, I've got people coming over tonight.

Think of some possible situations that you would use each of these expressions in. Decide with your teacher when each expression would be appropriate and what you might say before and after.

1.9   *Exercise*

Make up conversations from the cues below, using expressions presented in 1.8. Follow this pattern:

A: I'm going to have some people over for dinner tomorrow night. Would you like to join us?
B: Oh, I'm afraid I'm busy tomorrow night.
A: Some other time maybe?
B: Sure. Thanks for asking me.

movie	picnic
play	football game
drink	swimming
lunch/dinner	drive
dancing	roller skating

1.10   *Exercise*

Get up again and try to make a date with the people you contacted earlier. One way to begin might be: *Oh, it's nice to see you again. How are you?*
Remember that if you become too friendly or emotional, the person you are talking to may think you want a favor or that you are not sincere. Of course, if you are not friendly enough, you will sound rude.
Keep experimenting and practicing until you feel comfortable with the expressions in this unit.

Discuss each of the following with your teacher before you do them yourself. Decide on the best way to approach each one:

1 Imagine two people meeting for the first time and write the conversation between them in dialogue form.

2 Imagine that you are writing your first letter to an American pen pal. Introduce yourself, so that he or she has an impression of what kind of person you are.

3 Write a letter inviting an American acquaintance to spend the weekend with your family.

2 Asking for information: question techniques, answering techniques, getting more information

---

2.1 Conversation 📼

Sue: Hi, Anne!

Anne: Oh hi, Sue!

Sue: Uh listen, I was wondering if you could help me. Do you happen to know where there's a good place to buy art supplies?

Anne: I'm not really sure. Hey, let me think for a minute. Oh yeah, there's that new place, Mixed Media – you know, it's down on Main Street?

Sue: Mm, I don't know that store – exactly where on Main Street?

Anne: Well, you know where the new vegetarian restaurant is – it's right up a block.

Sue: Oh yes, I know where you mean now.

Anne: Hey, I hope you don't mind my asking, but are you taking up painting? *Joking*

Sue: [*laughs*] Are you kidding? I can't paint! I'm just asking for my sister's son. He's really into it.

Anne: Ah . . . oh, I see. Hey, are you still doing your photography? You're really good at that.

Sue: Yeah, that's the one thing I really enjoy.

Anne: Hey listen. This may sound like a dumb question, but can you get any good pictures on an automatic?

Sue: No, no, no, now that's a very interesting question. Automatics are OK, except for special effects, or stop action.

Anne: Oh, and it . . . listen, there's something else I was wondering about – like, should you do all your own developing?

Sue: Oh no! You don't have to develop your own. You can get good prints if you send them out.

Anne: No kidding! Could you tell me something more about it – like, if I was going to set up a darkroom, what would I really be using it for – what kind of equipment would I need?

Sue: Oh well, you'd need your enlarger, and . . . and chemicals, but actually developing is only cheaper when you're doing a lot of enlargements.

Anne: Oh, I see. Can I ask if you're making any money at it?

Sue: [laughs] Well, I'm making enough, and . . . well, it's tax time, so that's something I'd rather not talk about.

Anne: [laughs] I really understand. Well, I got to be getting along now, so, so long!

Sue: Bye!

2.2 *Presentation: question techniques*

A conversation often depends on questions to keep it going in the direction you want it to go. The one who asks the questions in a conversation usually controls the conversation. Various techniques may be necessary to get different kinds of information from different people. Most people are very polite when they ask a stranger about something – if you are more direct, you may appear to be rude. Anyway, personal questions have to be expressed very politely. Here are some useful opening expressions you can use to lead up to questions:

I was wondering if you could help me. I'd like to know . . .
I wonder if you could tell me . . .
This may sound like a dumb question, but I'd like to know . . .
Excuse me, do you know . . . ?
I hope you don't mind my asking, but I'd like to know . . .
Something else I'd like to know is . . .

Decide with your teacher when such expressions might be appropriate. They are also useful as "hesitation devices" to give you time to prepare your thoughts!

2.3 *Exercise*

Make notes for yourself about five pieces of general information and five pieces of personal information you would like from your teacher. Take turns asking your teacher questions. Be careful to be very polite when asking personal questions. When you have finished, ask a friend similar questions.

Presentation: answering techniques

You may often need to delay answering a question while you think for a moment or check on your facts. Here are some useful techniques for delaying your answer:

Well, let me see ...
Well now ...
Oh, let me think for a minute ...
I'm not sure; I'll have to check ...
That's a very interesting question.

On the other hand, you may not know the answer or you may want to avoid giving an answer for some reason. Then you can use expressions like:

I'm not really sure.
I can't answer that one.
I'm sorry, I really don't know.
I've got no idea.
I'd like to help you, but ...
That's something I'd rather not talk about just now.

Think of some situations when you might use these expressions. Decide with your teacher when they would be appropriate.

2.5   *Exercise*

Now your teacher is going to ask you questions like the ones you asked in 2.3. Try to delay or avoid answering them.

2.6   *Communication activity*

Work in pairs. You will be getting information about the career of the Beatles. One of you should look at activity 40 while the other one looks at activity 109.

Presentation: getting more information

When you ask people questions, they often don't give you enough information right away. Then you have to ask them for additional information – you may want more details or you may not be satisfied with the answers they have given. Here are some techniques for getting the extra information that you want:

Could you tell me some more about ... ?
Would you mind telling me more about ... ?
I'd like to know more about ...
Something else I was wondering about was ...
Sorry, that's not really what I mean. What I'd like to know is ...
Sorry to keep after you, but could you tell me ... ?
Sorry, I don't quite understand why ...

Decide with your teacher when these expressions would be used and what might be said before and after.

2.8 ## *Exercise*

Get your teacher to give you as much information as possible on his or her:

education   favorite way of spending evenings
professional career so far   favorite way of spending weekends
favorite vacation spot

Try to get as many details as you can.

2.9 ## *Communication activity*

Work in groups of four (or three). What do you know about the inventors of these common objects?

Each of you is an expert on one of them. Student A should look at activity 99, student B at activity 92, student C at activity 44, and student D at activity 8.

2.10   *Consolidation exercise*

Work in pairs or small groups. Ask each of your partners to give you as much information as possible about his or her:

town
country
job or field of study
family and friends
hobbies
sports activities

or about a place in the United States that he or she knows

Deal with each topic by asking your partner(s) questions.

2.11   *Written work*

This section concentrates on asking for information in letters. Discuss with your teacher the special techniques that you will need for this exercise.

1 Write a letter to the Hotel Romantica to find out about their prices and facilities. You are thinking of taking your family there for two weeks.

2 Write a personal letter to an old colleague or classmate about how he or she is getting along and how life has changed since you last saw each other three years ago.

When you have done 1 and 2, deliver your letters to another student, who will then write replies to the letters.

3 Getting people to do things: requesting, attracting attention, agreeing and refusing

---

Conversation 🔲

Bob: Well, what do think of this, Mary? Do you like this restaurant?
Mary: Oh, honey, it looks very nice. Oh, look, let's see if we can sit over
           there by the window so we can look at the water!
Bob: Oh yeah, sure. Uh, hm, excuse me miss, could we have a table
           over there by the window?
Waitress: Nuh, I'm sorry, we're closing that section. Would you mind sitting
           over here?
Mary: Oh . . . oh, all right, sure.
Bob: Mm . . . Well, OK, I wonder what's on the menu.
Mary: I'm starving.
Bob: We don't have a menu. There's not one on this table.
Mary: Oh.
Bob: Mary, d'you think you could, uh, ask those people over there . . .
Mary: Oh sure, honey. Just a minute. Um, excuse me, I wonder if we
           could . . . oh, I'm sorry . . . honey, they don't have one either.
Bob: Oh?
Mary: Oh, I'll ask the waitress. Waitress! Um, we'd like a menu
           please.
Waitress: Oh, I'm sorry. Yes of course, here you are.
Mary: Thank you.
Bob: Thanks. Ah, miss, could you tell me, what's the "soup of the
           day"?

Waitress:	Well, the "soup of the day" is cream of asparagus.
Mary:	Oh.
Bob:	Ah. Well, could you tell me the . . . about your "specials"?
Waitress:	Oh. Well, the "special" today is spaghetti.
Bob:	Uh-huh. Well, if you were going to be eating here yourself, what a . . . what would you have? What's really good?
Waitress:	Mm . . . I'd recommend the steak . . .
Bob:	Steak.
Waitress:	. . . we have really good beef here, yeah . . .
Mary:	OK. Well, give me a couple of minutes to think about it, OK?
Waitress:	OK. I'll be right back.
Mary:	OK.
Bob:	Thanks.

3.2   *Presentation: requesting* 🖭

When you want someone to do something for you, there are many English
expressions you can use. Some of these expressions are too polite for
some situations. Other expressions sound rude in particular situations.
The right expression to use depends on:

a) how difficult, unpleasant, or urgent the task is, and
b) who you are and who you are talking to – the roles you are playing.

See what happens in this example of too much politeness in an urgent
situation:

Imagine what will happen in this rude request for a favor from an important
man!

Here are some useful ways of requesting. They are marked with *stars*, according to how polite they are.

Informal (handwritten margin note)

★ *Hey, I need some change.*
I'm all out of change.

★★ *You don't have a quarter, do you?*
Have you got a quarter, by any chance?
Could I borrow a quarter?

★★★ *You couldn't lend me a dollar, could you?*
Do you think you could lend me a dollar?
I wonder if you could lend me a dollar.

★★★★ *Would you mind lending me five dollars?*
If you could lend me five dollars, I'd be very grateful.

★★★★★ *Could you possibly lend me your typewriter?*
Do you think you could possibly lend me your typewriter?
I wonder if you could possibly lend me your typewriter.

Very formal (handwritten margin note)

★★★★★★ *I hope you don't mind my asking, but I wonder if it might be at all possible for you to lend me your car.*

Decide with your teacher when you would use these request forms. Can you add any more forms to the list?

3.3 Exercise

Because your tone of voice is extremely important when you ask someone to do something, this section should be done with your teacher. You may need to be corrected frequently at first.
Treat your teacher as an equal whom you know but do not know very well. Ask him or her to lend you these things:

nickel	pen	comb
quarter	stopwatch	dictionary
$5	bicycle	kleenex
$100	piece of paper	nail file
$500	typewriter	car

Now ask him or her to do these things:

open the window halfway – open it all the way – close it
open the door – half close it – close it
move his or her chair – move it elsewhere – move it back to its
    original position
explain these words – *rude, appropriate, urgent*
get you a drink, a sandwich, a newspaper, some cigarettes
give you a cigarette, a light, a pencil, a recommendation

3.4 Communication activity

Begin working in pairs. In this activity you will be asking people to do different things for you. One of you should look at activity 80 while the other one looks at activity 47.

3.5 *Exercise*

So far you have practiced different forms of request that depended mainly on how difficult, unpleasant, or urgent the task was. We are now going to look at the second variable: the roles of the participants. Your teacher is going to play a number of different roles (see below), each one for a few minutes. Get him or her to do some of the same things you wanted done in 3.3. By the way, there may be some tasks that you shouldn't ask these people to do!

the receptionist in a hotel
your boss in an office
your secretary in an office

your best friend
your father (or mother)-in-law-to-be
an elderly stranger
a child

3.6 *Communication activity*

Work in pairs. You will be asking different kinds of people to do different things for you. Student A should look at activity 41 while student B looks at activity 61. All those playing student B will have to meet to divide up the roles mentioned in their activity.

3.7 Presentation: attracting attention, agreeing and refusing

It is sometimes difficult to attract the attention of someone who is busy doing something. Here are some expressions you can use to get someone's attention in a polite way:

Uh, excuse me . . .
Pardon me . . .
Uh, Mr. Jones . . .
Hey, Betty . . .

People try to attract your attention when they want to ask you to do something. You may then want to agree to do it or refuse to do it.

To agree:

OK.
Sure.
I'd be glad to.
Yes, of course.

To refuse:

I'm sorry, but . . .
I'd like to, but . . .
I'd really like to help you out, but . . .

Be careful to be polite when you refuse requests. North Americans often give an excuse in order not to hurt the listener's feelings. These excuses are sometimes called "little white lies," but of course they should not involve serious or obvious lying.

3.8 Exercise

Make up conversations from the cues below, using expressions presented in 3.7. Follow this pattern:

A: Excuse me . . .
B: Yes?
A: I was wondering if you could lend me your dictionary – I'm doing my homework.
B: I'm sorry. I'm using it right now. Maybe later.
A: Oh, that's OK. Thanks anyway.

open the door	check the spelling in a letter for me
lend me the newspaper	type an application form for me
give me a cigarette	give me a ride home
get me a cup of coffee	arrive on time
pass the salt	write more clearly
tell me the time	speak more slowly

Try to use a variety of expressions!

3.9 *Communication activity*

Work in pairs. You will be asking strangers to do different things for you. One of you should look at activity 53 while the other one looks at activity 1.

3.10 *Communication activity*

Work in groups of two or three on three different situations where someone needs help. Student A should look at activity 93 while students B and C look at activity 17.

3.11 *Written work*

Discuss these ideas with your teacher before you start writing.

1 You have a rich uncle. You want him to lend you some money so that you can buy a new car. He knows you smashed up your old one. Write him a letter asking him to lend you the money. Give reasons.

2 You have a nephew (or niece) who always spends too much money. You have just received a letter asking for more money. Reply as you think fit.

3 Write in dialogue form the first part of one of the conversations you had in 3.10.

4 Talking about past events: remembering, describing experiences, imagining What if ...

John: Say, Bob ...

Bob: Yeah?

John: Didn't you once almost get married, a long time before you met Mary?

Bob: Oh, yeah, I did. That was ... uh ... I'll never forget that. That was in, um ... Philadelphia, of all places. I was twenty-one. I was, uh, I'd knocked back a few drinks, you know, so I was feeling pretty good by this time, and uh, I was out on the road, you know with ... working with some people, and there was this particular woman that I really liked – blond, beautiful – real nice woman. So we were standing out there in front of the hotel, about two in the morning, and I said, "What do you think about getting married?"

John: Yeah? And what happened next?

Bob: Uh, she said something about how she was really flattered by the offer, and um ... then the next thing I did was to, uh, say, "Well

21

think about it," and, uh, I guess she did. We talked about it later
on, but nothing ever came of it. Great woman! Real nice.

John: What would you've done if she'd said yes? Would you have gone
through with it? I mean, you were a little drunk then; maybe, uh
... if you'd sobered up ...

Bob: Yeah, yeah, huh, that's uh, it's hard to say, but I ... I think I, I would
have. I think I would have. But uh ... later on I would probably
have regretted it, you know, because we were really so different.

4.2 Presentation: remembering

Different sorts of questions can help people to remember things that happened. If you want specific information, you have to use questions like
these:

What happened next?   *Why didn't you ... ?*
Did you ... before that?   *How did you feel when ... ?*
What were you doing while ... ? *Did you think of ... ?*
Then what did you do?

Decide with your teacher when these questions would be most useful.
Think of examples.

Before doing the exercises, look at some expressions that are often used to
answer specific questions:

As far as I can remember ...   *Before that ...*
I remember it very clearly.   *The next thing I did was to ...*
After that ...   *So then I think I ...*

Decide how these answers could continue.

4.3 Exercise

Do you remember your first day at school? Can you remember
   any details?
Do you remember your first big trip to another city or state? Can
   you remember much about it?
Do you remember the first time you drove a car all by yourself? What
   can you remember?

Try to get everyone in the class (including your teacher) to answer each
of these questions – then help them to remember more details by asking
questions like the ones suggested in 4.2.

4.4 Communication activity

Work in pairs. You will find out what your partner did yesterday. (For this
activity, you and your partner will know each other slightly, but you will
not be close friends.) One of you should look at activity 22 while the other
one looks at activity 79.

4.5   Exercise

Work in small groups. Help each other to remember as much as possible about these topics:

your last vacation
the most exciting sports event you've ever seen
your earliest memory
the last time you were interviewed

Report the most amusing or interesting details to the rest of the class.

4.6   Presentation: describing experiences

It is often interesting to find out about other people's experiences. Here are some questions which can help people to remember experiences which they had almost forgotten:

Did you ever ... ?
Tell me about the time you ...
I hear you once ...
Didn't you once ...
You've ... , haven't you?

And you can begin talking about your experiences like this:

Oh, that takes me back.
I'm not sure I can remember all the details, but ...
I'll never forget the time I ...
That reminds me of the time I ...
Well, as I remember it ...

Decide with your teacher how you could continue from these openings.

4.7   Exercise

Divide into groups of three or four. In each group, ask each other questions to help you to remember some funny or unpleasant experiences:

an unusual job you once had
a crime you witnessed or were the victim of
the longest or worst trip you ever took
an accident you saw or that happened to you
your driving test or first driving lesson
an unusual coincidence that you know about

Report the most interesting story to the rest of the class.

Often when we are recalling past events or experiences, we think about "what might have happened." Coincidences happen, we make decisions, things just happen – but what would have happened if the situation had been different?

Here are some ways of encouraging people to imagine:

What would you have done if ... ?
What would have happened if ... ?
How would you have felt if ... ?

Here are a few possible ways of beginning answers:

Oh, I don't know, I guess I would have ...
Hard to say, but I think I would have ...
Well, of course, I could have ...

Make sure you know how to pronounce these expressions, as well as when to use them.

4.9 *Exercise*

Think of four or five very different places in the world. What would have been *different* about your life so far if you had been born and brought up there? Talk about these aspects of your life with the rest of the class:

childhood   medical care
education   employment opportunities
family life   entertainment

Try to use some of the expressions introduced in 4.8.

4.10 *Exercise*

Here are a number of important events that have changed the history of the world. In groups of three or four, talk about what might have happened if these events had not taken place. Try to imagine *several* consequences of each event and what would have happened if all these things had not happened.

2,000,000,000 BC	First life on earth.
20,000 BC	First writing.
8,000 BC	Wheel invented.
AD 800	Paper money first used.
1327	Guns first used in battle.
1455	First book printed by Gutenberg in Germany.
1492	Columbus discovered America.
1556	Tobacco introduced to Europe.
1815	Napoleon defeated at Waterloo.
1818	Karl Marx born.
1865	Lincoln abolished slavery in United States.
1875	Bell invented the telephone.
1879	Edison invented the electric light.
1903	Wright Brothers' first powered flight.
1908	Ford started mass production of Model-T car.
1917	Revolution in Russia.
1926	Baird invented television.
1945	First use of atomic bomb in war.
1969	Armstrong stepped onto the moon.

When you have finished, report your most interesting ideas to the rest of the class.

4.11 Consolidation exercise

In small groups, talk about the vacation you remember best. Find out as much as you can about each other's vacations – including the things that might have gone wrong.

4.12 Written work

Discuss these ideas before you begin writing:

1 Write a letter to a friend about a trip you went on recently, or about the day you described in 4.4, or about what you did last weekend.

2 You saw one of these people at a party, but you were too shy to talk. Write down what might have happened and what you would have said if you had felt more confident.

3 Begin a little story with this opening line:
I'll never forget the day ...

5 Conversation techniques: hesitating, preventing interruptions and interrupting politely, bringing in other people

---

5.1 Conversation

Sue: You know, John, I feel that the developers are using up the best farmland building high-rises ...

John: Mm.

Sue: Nuh, in fact, I just joined this group – it's called The Citizens Against Overdevelopment – and they have a really good point ...

John: Yes, you're right, but ...

Sue: Oh, but another thing. I mean, of course we need places for people to live, but do they have to take some of the best farmland to build it?

John: Well, I know, but let's face it, we have more people, and they need housing, and industry has to be developed ...

Sue: Yes, but the way I see it is you don't have to take the best farmland to build high-rises ...

Mary: You know, Sue, I think you've got a good point there. Now, now John, what you were saying is right too, but I think if ... well, if everybody just got together and talked about it, I think everything would work out.

Sue: Well, see, the thing is, is that the developers have had their way long enough, and it's ...

Mary: That's right.

Sue: ... time for people to fight back!

Mary: Yes.

John: Bob, you've been very quiet up to now. What d'you think about all this?

Bob: [*laughs*] Well, I, you know, uh ... the thing is, uh, John, uh ... I pretty well like to mind my own business, and uh [*laughs*] ...

Sue: You mean you're not interested in politics?

Bob: Uh, well no, I'm, I'm, you know, well, I'm really, uh ...

Mary: I'm sorry to interrupt, everybody, but it's time for coffee!

5.2   *Presentation: hesitating*

Hesitation is a natural part of using a language – for those learning English as well as for native speakers. Very fluent speakers don't hesitate very often. But most people have to hesitate now and then during a conversation. Silence is not a good way to hesitate. Silence causes embarrassment and confusion. Silence also lets other people take over the conversation.

Here are some useful expressions you can use to fill the silence and to give you time to organize your thoughts and decide how to express them.

um	*how can I put it*
uh	*it's like this, you see*
well	*sort of*
well, let's see now	*uh* lengthened to *uh-uh*
in fact	*um* lengthened to *um-m*
you see	*the* lengthened to *th-uh-uh*
you know	*well* lengthened to *we-ell* or *we-ll-ll*
the thing is	

Decide with your teacher when these hesitation devices might be useful. You may have strong feelings about "bad English" – get them off your chest before you begin the exercise!

5.3   *Exercise*

Give a one-minute, totally unprepared talk to the rest of the class on one of these subjects. Choose the subject you know *least* about! The idea is to keep talking constantly and *not* be silent while you are thinking. In fact for this exercise you should try to give as little information as possible! The best way to start is *Well, I've been asked to talk about ...*

babies	hitchhiking	nudism
breakfast	the sun	classical music
trees	the moon	literature
coffee	communism	national politics
drugs	tourism	royalty
electricity	vegetarianism	insects

Make sure you and the others in the class are using a variety of hesitation devices – not just *um* all the time!

5.4 Presentation: preventing interruptions and interrupting politely

Even if you pride yourself on being a "good listener," there will be times when you want to keep talking and not be interrupted. Here are some useful techniques for you to try to prevent interruptions:

There are three points I'd like to make ...
(You can't be interrupted until you have made all three!)
Even though ...
(You can't be interrupted until you have spoken two clauses.)
And another thing ...
(You can't be interrupted until you have added a sentence.)
Pausing in the middle of a sentence, not between sentences.
(You can't be interrupted until you have completed your sentence.)

If you want to interrupt politely when another person is speaking, you need to be alert for suitable opportunities. This may take a lot of practice. If you break into the conversation at the wrong time, you may be considered aggressive. The end of a sentence is often a safe place to break in – but not always (see above!). Here are some useful techniques for interrupting:

If I could just come in here ... (formal)
Sorry to interrupt, but ...
Um ... *um* ... *um* ... (repeated until the speaker lets you speak)
By the way ... (to change the subject)
That reminds me ...
The way I see it ...

Discuss these techniques with your teacher and make sure your intonation and tone of voice are all right.

5.5 Communication activity

Work in groups of three or four. You will be discussing different aspects of "smokers' rights" and "work." Student A should look at activity 50, student B at activity 20, student C at activity 74, and student D at activity 107.

Actually, you probably don't want to appear to dominate people all the time! You may want to hear other people's views and make sure everyone gets a chance to speak in a conversation. A chairman at a meeting can just nominate speakers or point to them, but in a conversation it's better to use less direct methods:

Don't you agree, John?
What do you think, John?
You're very quiet, John.
I think John will agree with me when I say . . .
John's looking skeptical.
I don't know what John thinks, but . . .

Decide with your teacher what the effect of each of these techniques would be.

5.7   *Exercise*

Work in committees of four or five. Make sure that everyone gets a chance to state his or her views on each aspect of the following topic:

THE PROBLEMS OF OLD PEOPLE

When you are ready, report your discussion to the rest of the class. Then deal with the following topic in the same way:

TRAFFIC IN CITIES

5.8   *Communication activity*

Work in three groups. Each will conduct a committee meeting. Students in group A should look at activity 35, group B at activity 75, and group C at activity 101.

The techniques used in this unit are conversation techniques and are not generally used in writing, except when you are:

    writing a dialogue, or

    writing a friendly personal letter.

In both of these cases, conversational phrases only serve to make things sound more natural or intimate.

Discuss each of these ideas with your teacher before you start writing:

1a. Imagine you are on the phone with a friend. You are talking about what you both did today and yesterday. Write *only your side* of the conversation in dialogue form.

1b. Exchange one-sided dialogues with another student. Fill in the missing parts of the dialogue that you receive. Then get together with the other student and see if you both had the same ideas on how the conversations went.

2. Write a chatty personal letter to a good friend explaining why you didn't meet him or her as arranged yesterday. Invent some good excuses!

6 Talking about the future: stating intentions, discussing probability, considering What if ...

Conversation

Anne: Hi! Hi, Bob!
Bob: Hi ... hi.
Anne: Hey, when are you going on vacation?
Bob: Well, I'm hoping ... I think I'm going to go in March. I've got three weeks in March ... and then I've got another three weeks in September, so I'm hoping to get away at least one of those times.
Anne: Huh. You going to take Mary with you?
Bob: Sure.
Anne: Or are you going to, uh, you know, you going to take her with you on a vacation? You going away?
Bob: Yeah, yeah, well ... I don't think we'll have enough money to go away in March, but we're sure hoping to, uh, to travel in September.
Anne: Oh, really, where are you going to go, if you get out?
Bob: Well, you know, I want to go to Mexico. I've, I've never been there, and I just keep hearing all these great things about it. I, I don't know, uh, I haven't made up my mind if I'm going to, you know, uh, Acapulco or someplace else, uh ...
Anne: Oh god, it's sure to be fantastic – especially if you go in September – you can get those charters ...
Bob: Mm.
Anne: It's really cheap, and it's ...
Bob: Yeah.
Anne: ... beautiful down there.
Bob: Yeah, yeah, well maybe we could do that, but the costs keep going

up, you know, and there's still . . . so there's a chance we might not be able to go anywhere; we may just have to . . .

Anne: Yeah.

Bob: . . . pay the mortgage.

Anne: [*laughs*] Well, what would you be doing if you stayed back here?

Bob: Mm . . . I suppose I'd, I'd putter around the garden and uh, fix the doghouse, you know . . .

Anne: [*laughs*]

Bob: I gotta replace the eaves-troughing . . .

Anne: Yeah. Supposing you had all the money in the world. Then where would you go?

Bob: Me? I'd go to the South Pacific.

Anne: Oh god . . .

Bob: Yeah.

Anne: Right . . . all right . . .

Bob: Where're you going to go this year?

Anne: Oh, I wouldn't be surprised if I head down to Las Vegas. If you're going to run out of money, that's one place to do it quick!

Bob: Right.

Anne: [*laughs*]

6.2 *Presentation: stating intentions*

Nothing is totally certain about the future. We can try to foresee events, we can make plans and state our intentions – but we can never be sure what will actually happen.

Here are some ways of stating intentions and showing how firmly we intend to do something. They are all phrased as answers to the question: *Are you going to . . . ?*

✓	YES, DEFINITELY:	*Nothing's going to stop me from . . . -ing . . .* *I'm sure going to . . .* *I'm certainly going to . . .* *I'm going to . . . , that's for sure.*
✓?	YES, PROBABLY:	*I think I'll . . .* *I may . . .* *I'm hoping to . . .* *I'd like to . . .*
??	PERHAPS:	*I'm thinking of . . . -ing . . .* *I thought I'd . . .* *I thought I might . . .* *I haven't made up my mind if I'm going to . . . or . . .*
✗?	NO, PROBABLY NOT:	*I don't think I'll . . .* *I don't really feel like . . . -ing . . .* *I'm not really planning to . . .*
✗	NO, DEFINITELY NOT:	*I'm certainly not going to . . .* *You won't catch me . . . -ing . . .* *I'm not going to . . . if I can help it.* *I'm definitely not going to . . .*

Decide with your teacher how you might use these expressions when talking about your plans for tonight. Be careful about your pronunciation and tone of voice!

6.3   *Exercise*

Look at this list of countries. Check the list through and decide how firmly you intend to visit or don't intend to visit each country in the next few years. Use the categories suggested in 6.2.

England	Switzerland
Mexico	Venezuela
Brazil	Portugal
China	Nigeria
Spain	Australia
Scotland	Jamaica
Ireland	Sweden
Italy	Japan

Tell the rest of the class about your intentions.

6.4   *Exercise*

Work in small groups. Talk about your intentions of visiting the countries that are nearest to your own country. Ask each other questions like:

Why?
Why not?
Why aren't you sure?
If you go there, what cities are you going to visit?

6.5   *Communication activity*

Form three groups. Each group will plan a trip. Group A should look
at activity 31, group B at activity 3, and group C at activity 143.

6.6   *Exercise*

Think about your plans for tonight, this weekend, and your next vacation. Get together with two or three other students and discuss your plans.
Talk about what you plan *not* to do, as well as what you intend to do.

6.7   *Presentation: probability*

Often we have no control at all over what will happen. But we can try to
judge whether something is likely to happen or not. We can even claim
to be absolutely certain.
Here are some ways of stating probability. They are all phrased as answers to the question: *Do you think it will . . . ?*

√	YES, DEFINITELY:	*Of course it'll . . .*
		It's going to . . . , no question about it.
		It's sure to . . .
		It's bound to . . .
√?	YES, PROBABLY:	*It'll probably . . .*
		I expect it to . . .
		I wouldn't be surprised if it . . . -ed.
		I bet it'll . . .
??	PERHAPS:	*I guess it might . . .*
		There's a chance it'll . . .
		It might . . .
		I suppose it might . . .
×?	NO, PROBABLY NOT:	*I doubt if it'll . . .*
		I don't think it'll . . .
		There's not much chance of it . . . -ing.
×	NO, DEFINITELY NOT:	*Of course it won't . . .*
		There's no chance of it . . . -ing.
		I'm absolutely sure it won't . . .
		It isn't going to . . . No way!

Decide with your teacher how you would use these expressions to talk
about *tomorrow's weather*. How important is the tone of voice that is used?
How much do you believe someone who claims to be absolutely certain
about something that is going to happen?

6.8 *Exercise*

Look at Madame Zoë's predictions for the future. Work in small groups and discuss how probable you think each of her predictions is. When you are ready, report your assessment of her predictions to the rest of the class.

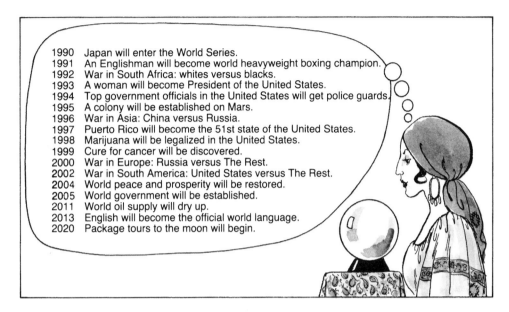

1990	Japan will enter the World Series.
1991	An Englishman will become world heavyweight boxing champion.
1992	War in South Africa: whites versus blacks.
1993	A woman will become President of the United States.
1994	Top government officials in the United States will get police guards.
1995	A colony will be established on Mars.
1996	War in Asia: China versus Russia.
1997	Puerto Rico will become the 51st state of the United States.
1998	Marijuana will be legalized in the United States.
1999	Cure for cancer will be discovered.
2000	War in Europe: Russia versus The Rest.
2002	War in South America: United States versus The Rest.
2004	World peace and prosperity will be restored.
2005	World government will be established.
2011	World oil supply will dry up.
2013	English will become the official world language.
2020	Package tours to the moon will begin.

6.9 *Exercise*

Prices of most things have gone up a lot in recent years. Can you predict how much these items will cost in five years' time?

box of matches
20 cigarettes
pair of shoes
stamp for letter overseas
local telephone call
cup of coffee

family car
1 gallon (or liter) of gasoline
color TV set
video recorder
quartz wristwatch
paperback novel

Begin in three groups, and decide on your prices. Then rearrange yourselves into three new groups to discuss your figures with students from the other groups.

6.10 *Exercise*

What changes do you expect to occur in the United States, in your country, and in the world during the next fifteen years? How different will everyday life be then?
Begin your discussion in groups; then report your predictions to the class.

Everything we have done so far in this unit is about the uncertain future. We can never be sure about what will happen. But sometimes we daydream about things that are *extremely unlikely* to happen and then imagine the consequences.

Here are some ways of encouraging someone to daydream:

What if you became a millionaire . . .
Supposing you came into a lot of money . . .
Imagine if you won a big lottery . . .

And you can ask someone to talk about the daydream with questions like these:

. . . what would you do?
. . . how would you feel?
. . . what would it be like?

The answers to these questions often begin like this:

Oh, I guess I'd . . .
Oh, I might . . .
Oh, I think I'd . . .
Me? I'd . . .

Notice that if we are talking about *possible* future events we normally say, for example:

A: *If you're* one of the winners, what *are you going to do* with the prize money?
B: Oh, I guess *I'll go* on a long trip.

Think of some examples of events that are either extremely unlikely or in fact possible. Make a question about each one.

6.12   *Exercise*

Make up conversations from the cues below, using expressions presented in 6.11. Follow this pattern:

  A: Supposing you got married tomorrow – how would you feel?
B: Oh, I guess I'd be really happy.
A: I think I would be too.

got married	met the Queen of England
had car stolen	saw a murder
found $20 bill	became a beauty queen
lost wallet	became homeless
failed exam	inherited a million dollars

Try to use all of the recommended expressions.

6.13   *Exercise*

Work in small groups. What would you do if you were in each of these situations? How would you feel? What would it be like?

Let your imagination take over and talk about the details of your life that would be different. Report your best ideas to the rest of the class.

6.14   *Communication activity*

Work in small groups. Decide on your own personal plans for the next few days *and* your ambitions for the future. Talk about events that you think will happen *and* things that probably won't happen.
Compare your own plans and ambitions with your partners' plans and ambitions.
When you have finished, look at activity 9.

6.15   *Written work*

1 Write a letter to a friend describing your plans for your next vacation.

2 Write a description of the world at some time in the future. Choose your own date.

3 If you became president of your country one day, what changes would you make?

7 Offering to do something, asking for permission, giving reasons

Conversation

John: Oh Anne, that was a wonderful dinner. That's the best meal I've had in a long time.

Anne: Oh thank you! Thank you very much.

John: Can I give you a hand with the dishes?

Anne: Uh-uh, don't bother. I'll do them myself later. Hey, would you like me to fix some coffee?

John: Uh, thanks a lot. I'd love some. Uh, would you mind if I smoke?

Anne: Why, not at all. Here, let me get you an ashtray.

John: Aw, thanks very much ... Oh Anne, I, I didn't realize you were such a good cook.

Anne: [*laughs*] Actually, I've only just learned how, you know. It's because I've been taking these courses.

John: Why, I can't cook at all, can't even boil an egg.

Anne: No kidding. Well, you know, if you want to, you could take a couple of classes over at Sheridan College and learn how to do it too.

John: Aw, thanks a lot, but ... I'm pretty busy these days.

Anne: [*laughs*]

John: Oh, I just remembered. Uh, I wonder if I could possibly use your phone.

Anne: Oo, I'm sorry, but it isn't working; it's out of order. Is it really important?

John: Well, you see, I have to call my foreman about tomorrow's work schedule. Uh, excuse me, would you, would you mind if I just went out for a few minutes? I'll give him a call from the phone booth on the corner.

Anne: Not at all. As long as you know your way back.

John: OK. I'll be right back.

7.2   *Presentation: offering to do something*

When something has to be done, you can ask someone else to do it, offer to do it yourself, or just do it without saying anything. If you want to be very polite when someone else is doing something, you can also offer to help. (This offer will often be refused.)

Here are some useful ways of offering to do something:

Let me get it for you.
Can I help you with that?
How about me getting it for you?
Would you like me to get it for you?
If you want, I could get it for you.
Any point in my getting it for you?

You might accept such offers with answers like:

Thanks a lot.
Oh, would you? Thanks.
That's nice of you, thanks.

Or refuse them by saying:

No, don't bother, I can do it myself.
No, it's all right. I can manage.
Thanks a lot, but I'm OK.

Decide with your teacher when you would use each of these expressions.

7.3   *Exercise*

Talk to your teacher and make some offers to help with his or her problems. Your teacher is bored, sick, lonely, thirsty, depressed, out of shape, hard up, hungry, and overworked. If you have time, do this with another student too.

7.4   *Communication activity*

Work in pairs. One person has some problems and the other person will offer to help. One of you should look at activity 91 while the other one looks at activity 63.

Sometimes you have to do more than just offer to do something – you may have to ask for permission to make sure you are allowed to do it. The expression to use depends on:

a) The type of task you want to do and the trouble you may have getting permission to do it.
b) Who you are and who you are talking to – the roles you are playing.

Here are some useful ways of asking for permission. The expressions get more and more polite as you go down the list:

I'm going to . . .
I thought I'd . . .
I'd like to . . .
OK if I . . . ?
Anybody mind if I . . . ?
Do you mind if I . . . ?
Is it all right if I . . . ?
Would it be OK if I . . . ?
Would you mind if I . . . ?
I wonder if I could possibly . . . ?
I hope you don't mind, but would it be possible for me to . . . ?

You usually give permission in just a short phrase, like:

OK.
Sure, go ahead.
Yes, I guess so.
All right.

And you refuse permission like this:

That's not a very good idea.
No, please don't.
I'd rather you didn't.
I'm sorry, but that's not possible.

Decide with your teacher when you might use each of these expressions. Give some examples of possible situations.

7.6 *Exercise*

Make a list of five things you would like to do but that you have to get your teacher's permission for. Ask for permission to do them – but watch out, your teacher may ask you why! Later your teacher will change roles and play the role of the head of the school, so then you may need to change the way you ask.

7.7 *Presentation: giving reasons*

When you ask people for permission, they are likely to ask you *Why?* Here are some useful ways of explaining your reasons:

Well, you see . . .
The reason is . . .
It's sort of complicated, but you see . . .
. . . and that's why I'd like to . . .
. . . and that's my reason for asking if I can . . .
Well, the thing is, . . .
It's because . . .

Discuss some ways to give reasons using these phrases (for example, if you wanted to borrow various things from your teacher).

7.8 *Exercise*

Make up conversations from the cues below, using expressions presented in 7.7. Follow this pattern:

 A: Would it be all right if I left for a minute? I have to make a phone call.
B: I'd rather you didn't – the thing is, this is a very important part of the lesson.
A: I see. OK.

(Imagine that you are talking to an acquaintance, rather than to a close friend.)

leave room	have coffee break
smoke my pipe	borrow umbrella
borrow car	use phone
take day off	watch TV
open window	borrow book

7.9 *Communication activity*

Work in pairs. One person will ask for permission to do things while the other person plays different roles. One of you should look at activity 11 while the other one looks at activity 56.

7.10   *Communication activity*

Work in groups of three. One of you (student A) is about to move into a new apartment and a lot of things need to be done. You each have a whole day free to do the work together.

Student A should look at activity 105, student B at activity 73, and student C at activity 19.

7.11   *Written work*

Discuss these ideas with your teacher before you start writing:

1 A friend of yours is leaving the country unexpectedly. Write a letter offering to help with last-minute packing, travel arrangements, etc.

2 Write a letter on behalf of your class to the park superintendent of your city requesting permission to hold a barbecue in a local park. Then "deliver" it to another student, who will write the park superintendent's reply.

3 Write a letter to a friend who owns a weekend cabin, asking him or her if you can spend a few days there with some friends. Then "deliver" it to another student, who will write your friend's reply.

8 Giving opinions, agreeing and disagreeing, discussing

Conversation 🔲

Sue: Well Ken, if you ask me, there's too much violence on television. Why, killing seems normal now.

Ken: Uh Sue, I'm not sure if I agree with you. I've never read any proof that supports your claim.

Sue: Oh Ken, it's common sense. The point is, is if you keep seeing shootings and muggings and stranglings, you won't care if it happens on your street.

Mary: I think that's interesting.

Ken: Maybe, but ... I've never met people that are that apathetic about violence.

Sue: Oh I'm sorry, I don't see what you mean. Would you mind explaining that point?

Ken: Let me put it another way, Sue. The people on my street – they're not influenced by what happens on television.

Sue: Oh, but people may care about violence on their street, but not about violence in general.

Ken: Wouldn't you say that . . . television is just a passive way of letting off steam?

Sue: Oh Ken, that's exactly what I mean! People watching violence to cool off proves my point – they get used to violence!

Mary: I think that's a good point, Sue. I mean, Ken, don't you see what she's saying?

Sue: Yes! There's got to be a better way to cool off!

Mary: I agree. Well, like talking with friends, or sports, or reading, or . . .

Ken: I agree with you, Mary. Anyway, TV's really boring, so why argue about it?

Sue: [laughs] I agree with you there.

Mary: [laughs] That's true.

8.2 *Presentation: giving opinions*

When you are taking part in a discussion it is useful to have techniques up your sleeve for getting people to listen to you and to give yourself *thinking time* while you arrange your ideas. Here are some useful opening expressions (they get more and more formal as you go down the list):

INFORMAL *If you ask me . . .*
You know what I think? I think that . . .
The point is . . .
Wouldn't you say that . . . ?
Don't you agree that . . . ?
As I see it . . .
I'd just like to say that I think that . . .
FORMAL *I'd like to point out that . . .*

Decide with your teacher when these different expressions would be appropriate. Do you agree with the order they have been put in? Can you suggest more expressions?

8.3 *Exercise*

Make up conversations from the cues below, using expressions presented in 8.2. Follow this pattern:

A: How do you feel about big dogs?
B: Well, if you ask me, big dogs are a nuisance.
A: Why do you think that?
B: Because they eat a lot of food, and run around where they're not wanted, and . . .

big dogs	foreign travel
cats	learning a foreign language
daycare	downtown parking spaces
women drivers	transistor radios
capital punishment	children

Try to use new expressions each time!

8.4 Exercise

Work in groups of three. Find out each other's opinions on these subjects:

vacations   inflation
birthdays   air travel
Christmas   television
politeness   winter sports
lotteries   communism

Report your partners' opinions to the students in another group.

8.5 Presentation: agreeing and disagreeing

Here are some useful ways of agreeing or disagreeing with someone's opinion. Notice that you need to be very *polite* when disagreeing with someone in English – even someone you know quite well.

AGREEMENT: *Exactly.*
               I couldn't agree more.
               That's just what I was thinking.
               You know, that's exactly what I think.
               That's a good point.

DISAGREEMENT: *Yes, that's quite true, but . . .*
               I'm not sure if I agree . . .
               Well, you have a point there, but . . .
               Maybe, but don't you think that . . .

If we know someone *very well* we can disagree more directly using expressions like these:

Are you kidding?
Don't make me laugh!
Come off it!

8.6 Exercise

Here is a series of extreme opinions:

"Learning English is pointless."
"The United States is not a nice place to live."
"Football is boring."
"Marriage is out of date."
"Space travel is a waste of money."
"Strikes should be made illegal."
"All motorists should be forced to wear seat belts."
"The speed limit should be forty miles an hour on all highways."
"English is a very easy language to learn."

Make up conversations about each topic, using the expressions presented in 8.5. Follow this pattern:

A: It says here that learning English is pointless!
B: I'm not sure if I agree – I think it's probably a good thing to do.
A: Why do you say that?
B: Well, because English is a world language – you need it to communicate with people from other countries.
A: That's a good point.

8.7   *Communication activity*

Work in groups of three. Each person will present some strong opinions and the others will react. Student A should look at activity 70, student B at activity 30, and student C at activity 7.

8.8   *Presentation: discussing*

In a friendly discussion, you don't want to present your opinions so strongly that you start an argument! You can express your opinion in a more tentative way like this:

I sometimes think that ...
Well, I've heard that ...
Wouldn't you say that ... ?
Do you think it's right to say that ... ?
It's my feeling that ...

And you may want to ask other people to explain their point of view more exactly, using expressions like this:

I didn't follow what you said about ...
Sorry, I don't see what you mean.
I don't exactly see what you're getting at.
What exactly are you trying to tell me?

And other people may not understand what you say to them. So you may need to rephrase your own statements, beginning like this:

That's not exactly what I mean ...
Let me put it another way ...
Sorry, let me explain ...
Let me try that again ...

Decide with your teacher how you would use these phrases in a discussion about a topic in the news today.

8.9   *Communication activity*

Work in pairs. One of you will present some ideas and then both of you will discuss them. The topics are EXAMS and MARRIAGE. One of you should look at activity 142 while the other one looks at activity 102.

8.10   *Exercise*

Work in groups of about six students. Pick *one* of these topics and discuss it, making sure each member of the group gets a chance to speak:

pollution
fashions
tourism

Make notes on the points that are made.

8.11   *Consolidation exercise: debate*

Begin by choosing a topic that everyone is interested in. Then spend some time preparing your opinions about the topic (perhaps in small groups). Then choose a chairperson and two opening speakers who will discuss the topic from opposite points of view.
After the opening speakers have clearly presented their opposing opinions on the topic, the discussion is "open to the floor" and everyone else can give their opinions.

8.12   *Written work*

Talk about these ideas with your teacher before you write anything:

1 Your teacher has been asked to write a confidential report giving his or her opinion on your character and work. Write the report you would like to have.

2 From the notes you made in 8.10, write a report of the discussion.

3 Write your opinions about a topic that is in the news or a topic you have discussed in this unit.

9 Describing things, instructing people how to do things, checking understanding

---

Ken: Sue, this tape recorder, it looks like a spaceship! How does it work?

Sue: Well, the first thing you have to do is plug it in. There's no *on–off* power switch on this machine.

Ken: I see. Well, how do you open it?

Sue: Well, to open the cover, you press E, which means *eject*. After you've done that, you put the cassette in. Now be careful not to put the cassette in backwards. The tape should always be facing you.

Ken: Sorry. Can you say that again?

Sue: OK. You put the cassette in with the tape facing you. OK so far?

Ken: M-hm.

Sue: OK. Now you close the cover, and press P, which is for *play*, and you press it hard.

Ken: I see. Uh, what's that red button?

Sue: Oh, the red button is for *record*. Now don't press it while playing tapes because it'll erase the material that's already on there.

Ken: And, that's the *rewind*?

Sue: That's right.

Ken: And there's the *stop*.

Sue: Fine! I think you're ready to take it on your own!

Presentation: describing things

You often have to describe an object, a piece of equipment, a machine, or a gadget to people. You may have to do this because your listener is unfamiliar with the object or because you cannot think of the name for it. In describing an object we often have to answer questions like these:

What size is it?
What shape is it?
What color is it?
What's it made of?
What does it look like?
What's it used for?
How does it work?

Decide with your teacher how you would answer these questions in describing the objects around you in the classroom. Are there any other important questions missing from the list?

9.3

Exercise

Here are some objects and gadgets to describe. Try to give a detailed description, bearing in mind the questions suggested in 9.2:

pencil sharpener	tape recorder
can opener	wristwatch
calculator	zipper
egg timer	pair of skis
toaster	razor

Get other students and your teacher to help if you cannot find the right words.

9.4

Exercise

Very often we cannot find the right word for something. For example, take a ruler. If you did not know the name for it, you could ask someone:

What do you call that thing about twelve inches long made of plastic or metal? You use it to draw lines and measure things.

Make up more *What do you call that thing . . . ?* questions about items you might find in a house or in a car or in an office.

9.5

Exercise

Make a secret list of:

an electric gadget	something you use in your job
something in your pocket or purse	something you can eat
an item of clothing	

Describe the items on your list to another student. Do not say what the thing is called – let your partner work it out. If your first list turns out to be too easy, try making a more difficult one together with your partner and challenge the rest of the class.

9.6   *Presentation: step-by-step instructions*

There is not much difference between telling someone how something works and instructing them how to do it themselves. More detail is needed and more repetition, too. When giving instructions, we often link the steps together like this:

First of all you ...
The first thing you have to do is ...

After you've done that, you ...
The next thing you do is ...

Oh, and then don't forget to ...
Make sure you remember to ...
Oh, and be careful not to ...

The amount of detail and repetition usually depends on who you are talking to and how much they know already.
Decide with your teacher how you would continue after using the expressions above.

9.7   *Exercise*

Pick one of the items you described in 9.5. Explain to your teacher how to use it. However, your teacher is going to pretend to be less mechanical than he or she usually is. Your teacher is also going to play a number of different roles: an old lady, a child, a know-it-all, your boss.

9.8 Communication activity

Work in pairs. Each one of you will explain to the other one how to make something. One person should look at activity 52 while the other one looks at activity 104.

9.9 Presentation: checking understanding

If you are giving instructions to someone, you will probably have to check as you go along that your listener understands. Like this:

OK so far?
Are you with me?
Is that clear?
Do you see what I mean?

And your listener may need encouragement if you are instructing him or her how to do something. When you see that your listener has understood, you can say things like:

That's right. Now ...
Got that? Good! Now ...
Fine! Now ...

An encouraging tone of voice is very important if you want to sound helpful. While you are getting complicated instructions, you may have to interrupt and ask questions like these:

Sorry, but I don't really see why you have to ...
Sorry, can you say that again, please?
Excuse me, I'm not very clear about ...

9.10 Communication activity

The class is divided into an even number of pairs and the pairs are divided into two groups, A and B. Each pair will work out the instructions on how to do or make something and then explain them to another pair. The pairs in group A should all look at activity 51 while the pairs in group B look at activity 82.

9.11 Consolidation exercise

Make notes to prepare yourself to explain to the rest of the class (or large group):

1 How to get from the school to your house.
2 An activity connected with your hobby or your job. (Try to choose an activity that the others probably don't know much about.)

1 Write a description of an object or gadget as truthfully but as mysteriously as you can, so that your teacher cannot guess what it is until you show him or her a picture or diagram of it.

Often notes and diagrams are a more effective way to present instructions than sentence after sentence of detailed explanation. Discuss these ideas with your teacher before you start writing:

2 Use notes (and diagrams if necessary) to explain how to cook an egg the way you like it.

3 Use notes (and diagrams if necessary) to show how to prepare a dessert that you like very much.

10 Talking about similarities, talking about differences, stating preferences

---

10.1   *Conversation*

Ken: Hey John, that new Honda you've got is just beautiful.
John: Yeah, it's a nice car, isn't it? Yours is a lot fancier though. I really like those electric windows.
Ken: Yeah, but our cars have something in common. Uh, they're both blue!
John: That's right. But they don't have much else in common.
Ken: How many miles to the gallon do you get?
John: Oh, I get about forty in town, a little more on the highway.
Ken: Oh really? I don't get anywhere near that. I only get about . . . twenty.
John: Yeah, but look at the speed you got in that thing. You can, you can really take it up there; you can go quite fast with that.
Ken: Yeah, but . . . there isn't much difference nowadays in speed or power. You can only go fifty-five on the highway anyway.
John: That's true. But you got a lot more power – you can really accelerate.
Ken: As far as I'm concerned, the only reason I have a lot of power in my car is . . . so I can haul my trailer.
John: Well, of course, you got a lot more room in the trunk than I have, too.
Ken: Mm. Yeah, but small cars are cheaper to run in the city.
John: That's true. A Honda's a lot better for me because I do a lot of city driving.

Ken: And small cars are easier to find parking spaces for.

John: Yeah, but neither one is all that cheap to run when you think about the cost of insurance and maintenance . . .

Ken: Mm-hm.

John: . . . and parking tickets and everything else.

Ken: You know what, John? I think I have an answer.

John: What's that?

Ken: Let's take the bus.

10.2 Presentation: talking about similarities and slight differences 📼

Look at these statistics:

	New Hampshire	Vermont	Arizona	New Mexico
Area in square miles	9,304	9,609	113,909	121,666
Population	738,000	444,000	1,771,000	1,016,000
Highest mountain (height in feet)	Mt. Washington 6,288	Mt. Mansfield 4,393	Humphrey's Peak 12,633	Wheeler Peak 13,161
Largest city (population)	Manchester 88,000	Burlington 39,000	Phoenix 968,000	Albuquerque 297,000
Joined United States	1788	1791	Feb. 1912	Jan. 1912

You can point out similarities between these states like this:

In spite of the obvious differences in size and population, the states of the United States have *many things in common*. For example:

There *isn't much difference* between the area of New Hampshire and the area of Vermont, although Vermont is *a bit* bigger.

The dates when Arizona and New Mexico joined the U.S. are *more or less the same*, although New Mexico joined *just a little bit* earlier.

Humphrey's Peak and Wheeler Peak are *roughly similar* in height, but Wheeler Peak is *slightly* higher.

Both Mt. Washington *and* Mt. Mansfield are more than 4,000 feet high, but *neither one* is *all that* high compared to the Rocky Mountains, for example.

Manchester and Burlington have *something in common*: *neither one of them* is *anywhere near* as big as Phoenix.

Use sentences similar to the ones above to make some other comparisons between the four states. Write your best sentences down. How is your state or province or country similar?

10.3 *Exercise*

In small groups, compare the place where you grew up with the place where you are now (or a place where you'd like to be). What are the similarities in:

climate	food and drink
industry	agriculture
people	political climate
traffic	television
railways	education
scenery	family life
city life	clothes

Tell your partners about the similarities. Ask each other *In what way?* and *How do you mean?* questions.

10.4 *Exercise*

In pairs or small groups, find a topic that is of common interest – you might like to talk about different cars, stereo systems, movies, vacation resorts, cities, or clothes, for example. Discuss the similarities between them. Report your discussion to the rest of the class.

Look at these statistics:

	Rhode Island	Texas
Area in square miles	1,214	267,338
Population	950,000	11,197,000
Highest mountain (height in feet)	Jerimoth Hill 812	Guadalupe Peak 8,751
Largest city (population)	Providence 795,000	Houston 1,678,000
Joined United States	1790	1845

You can point out differences between these states like this:

In spite of the fact that they are both states of the U.S., Rhode Island and Texas have *very little in common*. For example:

Rhode Island *isn't anywhere near* as big as Texas – in fact, Texas is about 225 times bigger than Rhode Island!

The population of Rhode Island is *nowhere near* the population of Texas – in fact, Texas has about 12 times the population of Rhode Island.

Houston is *a lot* bigger than Providence – in fact it's twice as big.

There's *a large number of* differences between the people of Rhode Island and Texas – their accent, their attitudes, and even their behavior is *quite* different.

Point out some more differences between the two states, and between your own state, province, or country and Rhode Island or Texas. Write down your best sentences.

10.6   *Exercise*

In large groups, comment on the differences between the countries shown in these statistics:

	United States	Canada	Australia	New Zealand	United Kingdom
Area in square miles	3,615,122	3,851,809	2,967,909	103,736	94,512
Population	222,020,000	23,810,000	14,417,000	3,107,000	55,901,000
Highest mountain (height in feet)	Mt. McKinley 20,320	Mt. Logan 19,850	Kosciusko 7,316	Mt. Cook 12,349	Ben Nevis 4,406
Largest city (population)	New York 10,716,000	Toronto 2,865,000	Sydney 3,155,000	Auckland 806,000	London 7,379,000

Report your discussion to the other group(s).

10.7 *Exercise*

In small groups, compare again the place where you grew up with the place where you are now (or a place where you'd like to be). This time, what are the differences in:

climate	standard of living	system of government
people	breakfast	weights and measurements
scenery	public transportation	prices
food and drink	sports	driving rules and habits
family life	language	

Tell your partners about the differences. Ask each other *In what way?* and *How do you mean?* questions.

10.8 *Exercise*

Here are some ideas for a more general discussion. In small groups, talk about the differences and similarities between the following:

a vacation in a hotel	*versus*	a camping vacation
working in an office	*versus*	working in a factory
getting married	*versus*	staying single
life now	*versus*	life ten years ago
playing chess	*versus*	playing Monopoly
learning English	*versus*	learning *your* language

10.9 *Exercise*

Team up with another student and talk about your family, job, education, experiences, and interests. Try to find the similarities and differences between your life and your partner's life.

When you have enough information, change partners and report to someone else what you found out.

10.10 *Presentation: stating preferences*

Comparing things often involves making a choice. If we are comparing different cars, for example, we often state our preferences at the same time. Here are some useful ways of stating what you prefer:

As far as I'm concerned, the best . . .
From my point of view, the best . . .
I'd go for this one because . . .
I'd prefer that one because . . .
This one's better for me because . . .

Decide with your teacher how you would use these expressions to talk about different things to eat and drink. Perhaps look at a restaurant menu and decide what dishes to order.

10.11 *Exercise*

Look at the following descriptions of five major cities. Then, in groups of three or four, decide which place would be best for you:

a) for a long vacation
b) to work in
c) to visit for a few days

Explain why. You can make the exercise more exciting by having each person act as a "public relations officer" for one of the places.

	Population	Major industry	Major attractions	Weather
New York	10,716,000	Financial institutions	Largest city in the West	Humid; cold winter
Washington	2,900,000	Federal government	Many historical landmarks	Humid; winter not so cold
Houston	1,678,000	Space and oil industries	Astrodome; growing very fast	Humid; very hot summer
San Francisco	3,000,000	Seaport trading with Asia	Very varied population	Mild; some fog
Las Vegas	275,000	Gambling	Night clubs	Dry; very hot summer

10.12 *Consolidation exercise*

Look at the following three job ads. Talk with another student about their similarities and differences and which job you would like best. Decide what each job would involve – what kind of work, how much money, how much free time, how much worry, and so on.
If there is time, report your decision to the whole class.

SECRETARIAL   TYPIST

IT'S AN EXCITING . . .
PROFITABLE CAREER

Get ahead with a MATURE business attitude and stay ahead with the skill of the 80's— WORD PROCESSING. Mature Temps is prepared to help you learn the Xerox 860 and/ or Lexitron. Must type 55 wpm.

Call or stop by for information.

MATURE TEMPS, INC.
1899 L St. NW
833-8888

Swimming Pool Supervisors
— Various Locations, N.W.T. —

Pool supervisors are required in a number of Northwest Territories communities from June 1 to August 31.   Duties will include operating and maintaining above-ground pools and instructing aquatic activities, water safety and Royal Life Saving.

Experience is necessary and a valid Red Cross instructor certificate is required. Free, furnished accommodation is available.

Write to:
Recreation Division
Department of Local Government
Government of the N.W.T.
Yellowknife, N.W.T. X1A 2L9
Canada

Northwest
Territories

FEEL TRAPPED IN A NOTHING JOB?

BREAK OUT NOW

To a Challenging and Rewarding Career in

RETAIL MANAGEMENT

Strong Desire to Excel

Stock Purchase and Savings Investment Plans

Rapid Advancement Potential

Earnings Based on Personal Performance

College Grad or Retail Experience Preferred

Full and Part Time Opportunities Available

LET'S TALK IT OVER

Radio Shack

A DIVISION OF TANDY CORPORATION

AN EQUAL OPPORTUNITY EMPLOYER

10.13   *Written work*

Talk about these topics with your teacher before you start writing:

1 Your American pen-pal has never left home before. He or she is going to visit a foreign place you know well. Write a letter telling him or her what will be different there.

2 Write a paragraph describing the similarities and differences between two English-language newspapers you have read.

3 Write an account of the similarities and differences between this book and the last book you learned English from. Which do you prefer and why?

11 Making suggestions and giving advice, expressing enthusiasm, persuading

11.1 Conversation

Ken: Sue? Would you like a cigarette?
Sue: Thanks, but no thanks. I've quit.
Ken: D'you mind if I smoke?
Sue: No, I don't mind.
Ken: Huh. I'm really hooked on these cigarettes.
Sue: Well, I never smoked much, so I . . .
Ken: [coughs]
Sue: . . . thought it would be just better if I quit.
Ken: [coughs]
Sue: Say . . .
Ken: I smoke too much, I think!
Sue: That sounds like a really bad cough.
Ken: Mm. It does sound bad, I'm sure.
Sue: W-why, why don't you, uh, quit smoking Ken? It's bad for your health.
Ken: Sue, that's all very well, but . . . smoking means something to me. It's very important.

Sue: Listen, Ken, you could always, uh, cut down. Say to ten cigarettes a day.

Ken: Sue, that's easier said than done. But you see, smoking helps keep me calm.

Sue: Oh, I see what you mean. Well, have you ever thought about one of those, uh, tobacco substitutes?

Ken: Yech! You mean like lettuce?

Sue: [laughs]

Ken: I'd hate the taste. Anyway, you don't seem to understand that smoking helps keep me *slim*.

Sue: [laughs] I've heard that's true, but ... why don't you try chewing gum instead?

Ken: Mm. That's a good idea. But, if I chewed gum, I'd just be ... a, a nasty and irritable gum-chewer!

Sue: [laughs] Hey, listen, I've got a great idea. Why don't you go to a hypnotist?

Ken: That's a great idea. Now I've heard everything!

Sue: [laughs]

11.2 *Presentation: making suggestions and giving advice* ⌷

There are many ways of trying to get people to do things for their own good. The expressions you use depend on:

a) how difficult or unpleasant the action that you suggest is; and

b) who you are and who you are talking to – the roles you are playing.

Remember that suggestions or advice on personal matters are usually given only to close friends or when someone asks for advice. North Americans like to "do their own thing" and "mind their own business." But if you do want to make a suggestion, there are several useful expressions you can use. The ones below are in order – from polite suggestions to direct advice:

POLITE SUGGESTIONS *I was wondering if you'd ever thought of ...*
I think it might be a good idea to ...
Have you ever thought of ...
Don't you think it might be a good idea to ...
You could always ...
If I were you I'd ...
Why don't you ...

DIRECT ADVICE *You'd better ...*

Decide with your teacher when you would use these different expressions. How would you continue after each one?

11.3 *Exercise*

Your teacher is fed up with his or her present boring, unrewarding job. Suggest what your teacher should do. Help him or her with advice about evening, weekend, and vacation plans, too.

11.4 Exercise

Work in small groups. All of you are returning home soon and you have to take presents for your father, mother, sister, brother, grandmother, grandfather, best friend, fiancé(e), niece, nephew, etc. Ask for advice on what to bring each person.

When you have finished, report your discussion to another group.

11.5 Exercise

Work in small groups. What advice would you give to the people who wrote the following letters to an advice column in a newspaper?

I have just lost my job at age 43. I have a wife and 6 children to support and there seems to be no chance of getting another job. We don't want to move away from our friends and relatives. The other problem is that I am in debt. — I owe the bank $1,000. Can you give me any advice?

I am 25 years old and have a great job in an advertising agency, working for a very nice boss. The chances for a promotion look really good, but before I get too old I want to see the world. What I dream of doing is taking a year off and sailing around the world alone. The problem is that my boss says he can't keep my job open for me. My boyfriend is against me going too - he says it's too dangerous. What do you think I should do?

I am a housewife and a friend has just told me that my husband, Jim, is having an affair with his secretary. I'm worried because he often comes home late and says he has been working late at the office. Last weekend he said he had to go away to New York on business. I really don't know what to do: our two daughters are still in school and I don't want Jim to leave us. I just don't know what to do.

I am 55 years old and single. Now after all these years I have fallen head over heels in love. The girl I love is much younger than me — in fact she's 20 years old. She says she loves me but my relatives say she is just after my money. Her parents don't approve of me and want her to forget me. I don't want to be lonely the rest of my life. What should I do?

When you decide on what advice to give, report to the rest of the class.

11.6 Communication activity

Work in groups of four. Everybody will get advice from the others on some personal problems. Student A should look at activity 43, student B at activity 33, student C at activity 83, and student D at activity 5.

11.7 Presentation: expressing enthusiasm

When we give advice, we often need to "sell" our ideas. A natural salesman can use the "soft sell" approach and sell his product without putting any pressure on the customer. But most people have to show a lot of enthusiasm when they are trying to "sell" a product or an idea.
When we are enthusiastic, we use adjectives like these:

fantastic
incredible
great
really good
wonderful
sensational

They are often put into introductory phrases, like this:

I think it'd be a great idea to ...
I've got a fantastic idea ...
Hey, this is sensational! Listen to this ...
Hey! I've got this really good idea ...

Decide with your teacher how you would continue from these phrases. Practice your "enthusiastic" tone of voice, too!

11.8 Exercise

Begin in pairs and work out some ideas on each of these topics:

what to do in the next lesson
a good record to listen to
a good movie to see
a good book to read
how to practice English outside of school
how to become rich

When you are ready, make enthusiastic suggestions to the rest of the class.

11.9 Communication activity

Work in groups of three. You will decide what to do over the weekend. Student A should look at activity 13, student B at activity 119, and student C at activity 77.

11.10 Presentation: persuading

People do not always just accept suggestions and advice. They say things like this:

That's a good idea, but ...
That might be OK, but ...
What you don't seem to understand is that ...
I really don't think so, because ...

And then they state their doubts or objections. They may then have to be persuaded. You can often answer objections with phrases like these:

I see what you mean, but if ...
That's true, but if ...

Decide with your teacher how you would continue these openings if someone suggested, for example, climbing Mt. Everest.

11.11 Exercise

Your teacher smokes and drinks too much. Persuade him or her to stop or cut down and suggest some possible methods.

11.12 Communication activity

Work in pairs. You will have to decide where to go on your vacation. One of you should look at activity 141 while the other looks at activity 95.

11.13 Communication activity

Work in groups of four. Each one of you will have to try to convince the others to buy something. Student A should look at activity 72, student B at activity 29, student C at activity 4, and student D at activity 117.

Here are extracts from three letters you have received. Discuss them with your teacher before replying to them:

There's this very important exam coming up soon and I've really got to pass it. The trouble is I can't seem to get down to work. There are so many distractions and there's not much time left. I hope you can help,

Robert

looking for some ideas for a gift for his retirement. We've got about $200 to spend and we want to get something really special. Do you have any ideas? Please let me know.

Regards,
Richard

in fact I'm worried sick. He left two days ago and I'm sure he isn't coming back. He mentioned something about leaving the country and I'm afraid he might have gotten mixed up in something illegal. I can't go to the police in case he gets into trouble. What should I do?

Please write soon,
love,
Susan

12 Complaining, apologizing and forgiving, expressing disappointment

---

12.1   *Conversation*

Mary: Ken! Ken!

Ken: Hi, Mary. How are you?

Mary: Hi, I'm fine. How are you?

Ken: Good.

Mary: Listen, I, I'm not exactly sure how to put this, but, um . . . has my dog been digging up your backyard again?

Ken: I . . . don't think so. I, I haven't noticed.

Mary: Well, I sure hope he hasn't; I saw him running through your yard yesterday, and . . .

Ken: Oh, that's all right. I . . . don't worry about it. I don't mind your dog running through. Anyway, it . . . really is a shame that there's no place for the dogs to run in this neighborhood.

Mary: Oh, it's true, but, but that's still no excuse. I'll try and keep him on a leash so he doesn't bother you . . .

Bob: Ken, could I . . . could I talk with you for a minute?

Mary: Oh, hi, honey!

Ken: Hi, Bob.

Bob: Hi, Mary . . . Uh, Ken, I, I hate to bring this up, but . . . that new stereo system you got . . .

Ken: Yeah?

Bob You were playing it very late last night . . .

Ken: Yeah?

Bob: It kept me awake . . .

Ken: Oh, I'm sorry . . .

Bob: . . . a couple of hours.

Ken: I'm sorry, I, I didn't realize it was that loud.

Bob: Well, it was that loud, and it was pretty late, and . . . check with Mary if you don't believe me . . .

Mary: Huh, it's true, it, it was a bit loud, but, uh, it wasn't really bad . . .

Ken: I'm very sorry. I, I didn't realize it. I promise I'll keep it down in the future.

Bob: Oh, it's no problem; it's OK. You know, it only happened once.

Mary: I sure am glad we've straightened everything out.

12.2   *Presentation: complaining* 🔲

A direct complaint in English often sounds very rude. To be polite we usually "break the bad news gently" and use expressions like these before we actually come to the point:

I wonder if you could help me.
Look, I'm sorry to bother you, but . . .
There's something you could help me with.
I hate to have to say this, but . . .

It is safer to make a complaint politely with the above expressions than to say, for example:

Look John! I wish you'd get to class on time in the future.
or
I've just about had enough of you coming in late.

It is often not enough to just say *"Sorry"* and promise it won't happen again. You may have to apologize more elaborately like this:

Oh, I'm awfully sorry.
I can't tell you how sorry I am.
I'm very sorry. I didn't realize . . .
I just don't know what to say.
I'm extremely sorry.

Decide with your teacher how you would use these expressions in, for example, conversations between a teacher and a student.

12.3   *Exercise*

You are all staying in a hotel and a lot of things have gone wrong. Make up conversations from the cues below, using expressions presented in 12.2. Follow this pattern:

Guest: Excuse me, there's something you could help me with.
Desk clerk: What seems to be the problem, sir?
Guest: There isn't any hot water in my room.
Desk clerk: Oh, I'm sorry. I'll have it looked after right away.
Guest: Thanks.

hot water   soup
heating   steak
pillows   coffee
TV   no ice
draft   slow service

12.4   *Communication activity*

The class is divided into two groups. The people in one group will complain about bad products to the people in the other group, who are all store-keepers. One group should look at activity 60 while the other group looks at activity 6.

12.5   *Communication activity*

Work in pairs on making and receiving complaints. You will be playing the roles of neighbor and friend, so be polite. Remember that neighbors and friends can get very upset by complaints.
One of you should look at activity 128 while the other one looks at activity 54. You will find it more convenient to stand up, so that for each conversation you can approach your partner at the beginning and walk away at the end.

12.6   *Presentation: apologizing and forgiving*

When you do something wrong, you save yourself a lot of trouble by apologizing first – before someone complains to you. In this case it may be even more essential to "break the bad news gently." Here are some useful opening expressions:

I'm not exactly sure how to put this, but ...
I've got to apologize for ...
I'm afraid I have something to tell you ...
Um, this isn't easy to explain, but ...

After someone has heard what you've done they may ask you to explain how it happened. They may then "let you off the hook" and forgive you, like this:

Oh, that's all right; don't worry about it.
It's not your fault.
Oh, never mind. It doesn't really matter.
Please don't blame yourself.

Decide with your teacher how you would use these expressions if, for example, you took your friend's dog out for a walk and it ran away for two hours.

12.7   *Exercise*

Make up conversations from the cues below, using expressions presented in 12.6. Follow this pattern:

A: I'm not quite sure how to put this, but you know that lawnmower you lent me ...
B: Yes.
A: Well, I'm afraid it broke and I'd like to fix it for you.
B: Oh, that's all right; don't worry about it – it hasn't been working right for quite a while.

transistor radio	hair dryer
stapler	vacuum cleaner
slide projector	electric kettle
tape recorder	sewing machine
electric mixer	alarm clock

12.8   *Communication activity*

Work in pairs. Each person will have some apologies to make. One of you should look at activity 67 while the other one looks at activity 36.

Sometimes unpleasant things happen which can't be blamed on anyone. But we may want to express our disappointment to others. Here are some useful ways of doing this:

I was really looking forward to . . .
It really is a shame that . . .
It's too bad that . . .
I'm disappointed that . . .
If only . . .
I wish . . .

Often disappointments have to be taken philosophically – we can't let things upset us too much. Here are some ways of reacting calmly and changing the subject:

That's life.
Can't help that.
That's not worth worrying about.
Let's not cry over spilled milk.
Well, you can't win them all.
So it goes.

Decide with your teacher how you would use these expressions if, for example, bad weather prevented you from going out for a picnic.

12.10   *Exercise*

Make up conversations about the situations below, using expressions presented in 12.9. Follow this pattern:

A: I was really looking forward to the game.
B: Me too. Too bad it was rained out.
A: Well, can't help that.
B: No, I guess not. What are we going to do instead?
A: Well, we could . . .

1 Football game is canceled because of rain.
2 Theater has "sold out" sign outside.

3 In a restaurant the first course was so big you couldn't eat the main course you both ordered.
4 You missed the party because you were sick.
5 Your car is being fixed at the garage – you can't go on the trip.
6 What you had at the restaurant was bad – what the others had looked delicious.
7 You had a headache, so you didn't enjoy the concert.
8 You were both on vacation and forgot your address books, so you couldn't send anyone a card.

12.11 *Communication activity*

Work in groups of three. Each person will give some disappointing news to the others. One of you should look at activity 148, another at activity 21, and the third at activity 62.

12.12 *Communication activity*

Work in pairs on giving some bad news to the host or hostess in the house where you are staying. One of you should look at activity 96 while the other one looks at activity 87.

12.13 *Written work*

Discuss the following ideas with your teacher before you write these letters:

1 You bought a cassette player by mail order two weeks ago and now it's not working. Send it back with a letter complaining to the company you bought it from.

2 You and your club went on a package tour. You ended up at a terrible hotel for two weeks. Write a letter to the tour operator complaining about the various things that went wrong and warning the operator that his company may lose a lot of business.

3 Your friend failed his final university exams. Write a letter to sympathize.

13 *Describing places, describing people*

Conversation 🔲

[*phone rings*]

Sue: Hello?

Mary: Hi, Sue. It's Mary, Mary Graham.

Sue: Oh hi, Mary. How are you?

Mary: I'm fine. How are you?

Sue: Fine.

Mary: Listen, um . . . I want to ask you some questions about Jim Wilson
      – you know him, don't you?

Sue: Sure.

Mary: What's he like?

Sue: Well, why are you asking about Jim?

Mary: Well, I want to try and get a part-time job at his store . . .

Sue: Oh, well Jim's a nice guy . . .

Mary: Mm-hmm.

Sue: I mean he'll give you decent hours, a decent wage, and plenty of breaks.

Mary: Well, that sounds good. Um, what does he look like? I've got to meet him at the Sunset Restaurant for lunch and I can't remember.

Sue: Oh, well he's about thirty-six . . .

Mary: Uh-huh.

Sue: . . . six-foot-two . . .

Mary: Right.

Sue: . . . oh, has dark, wavy hair with a little gray at the temples.

Mary: Oh, sounds kind of nice.

Sue: Mm.

Mary: Um, is he a, a formal kind of guy, or does he dress casually?

Sue: Oh, he rarely dresses casually. He always wears three-piece suits and ties – dresses very much in style.

Mary: Oh, I see, I better dress up then . . .

Sue: Mm-hmm!

Mary: Mm-hmm. Oh, listen, where's the Sunset Restaurant – is that the one near Hudson's?

Sue: Oh no! No, no no! That's the Sun*shine* Restaurant . . .

Mary: Right.

Sue: The Sun*set* Restaurant is on Oak Street.

Mary: That's right. Is it a nice place?

Sue: Oh, it's a wonderful place. Uh, rather expensive though.

Mary: Uh-oh.

Sue: Oh no, well, Jim'll probably pick up the bill.

Mary: [*laughs*] I hope so . . . Listen, how do I get there?

Sue: Oh, you taking your car?

Mary: Mm-hmm.

Sue: Well, you go up Main Street, to Broad . . .

Mary: Right.

Sue: . . . over on Broad – eight blocks – to Oak . . .

Mary: Oak.

Sue: . . . take a left on Oak Street . . .

Mary: Uh-huh.

Sue: . . . and then there's a big parking lot on the right, just about half a block after the turn . . .

Mary: Right.

Sue: . . . and it's right next to that.

Mary: OK. Was that a left or a right on Oak?

Sue: Left on Oak.

Mary: Left on Oak. I got it.

Sue: OK.

Mary: Wish me luck!

Sue: Oh, for sure! You call me and tell me what happens.

Mary: I will.

Sue: OK.

Mary: Thanks.

Sue: Bye.

Mary: Bye-bye.

You often have to describe places to people – a house or a building they haven't seen, a town or a city or a village they haven't visited, scenery or countryside they aren't familiar with, and so on. Here are some of the questions you may have to answer:

Where is it?
What does it look like?
How do you get there?
What's interesting or unusual about it?
What's nice, or not so nice, about it?

If it's a house or a building, you may also have to answer questions like these:

What other buildings are around it?
What's it used for?
How old is it?

Decide with your teacher how you would answer these questions when you are talking about:

the building you're in now and the buildings nearby
the city you're in now
the countryside near the city you're in now

13.3   *Exercise*

Look at the pictures on this page and on the next page.
Imagine that they are postcards you sent on your vacation. With your teacher's help, make a list of the words you need to describe each place, and then give a description with as much detail as possible.

13.4   *Exercise*

Work alone first and make a secret list of:

a well-known building
a town or city you know
a local landmark
a well-known street or avenue
an area or country you know

Then work in small groups and *without* saying *where* each place is, describe it to your partners. Get them to guess the name of the place after you have described it.

13.5   *Exercise*

Get together with two or three others and describe your favorite place to them. Try to make it sound as attractive as possible!

You often have to answer this question: *What's so-and-so like?* This does not usually mean giving a detailed description of a person's physical appearance. A better way to answer the question is to say what sort of person he or she is and perhaps to mention a few noticeable characteristics. Here are some of the characteristics you may use to describe people:

general personal impression
age
height, weight, build or figure
face, hair, eyes, complexion
clothes
personality
job
interests, sports, and hobbies
their life so far: achievements, family background . . .

Think of various people you know and decide with your teacher how you would describe them. Get the words you need by asking other members of the class or your teacher, or by using a dictionary.

13.7   *Exercise*

Look at the people in the pictures below and on the front cover of this book. How would you describe each of the people in the pictures?

13.8 *Exercise*

Look at everyone in the room very carefully for a couple of minutes. Then stand back-to-back with one of them and, *without looking*, describe each other. Keep going until everyone has had a turn.

13.9 *Exercise*

Work alone for a few minutes and make a secret list of:

a male movie star	another teacher
a female movie star	another student
a famous singer	someone nobody else in the class knows
a well-known politician	

When you are ready, work in small groups and get the others to ask you questions to find out the characteristics of the person you have in mind. Avoid answering questions that will allow the others to guess the name of the person too quickly.

13.10 *Consolidation exercise*

Begin by closing your eyes and trying to visualize:

your house and city	the people you work with
the members of your family	your friends

After a few minutes of silence, get together with two or three other students and describe to them the main characteristics of these places and people. Find out as much as possible about their homes and the people they know – try to form a clear visual impression of everything and everyone they describe.

Report one of your partners' most interesting or vivid descriptions to the rest of the class.

13.11 *Written work*

Discuss the following ideas with your teacher before you start writing.

1 Your teacher is arriving at the airport but you cannot meet the plane yourself. Write a description of your teacher so that someone else can go to meet the plane and will be able to recognize him or her.

2 You arranged to meet someone at a friend's house. Unfortunately, you can only remember the name of the street, not the number of the house. Write a description of the house so that your friend can find it.

3 Write a description of the most remarkable, or unpleasant, person you have ever met.

14 Telling a story: narrative techniques, handling dialogue, controlling a narrative

14.1 Conversation

Anne: Did I ever tell you about the time I got hit by a Datsun truck when I was driving my two-ton van?

John: No, you never did. What was that all about?

Anne: Well, what happened was, I was just outside of San Antonio, and this little Datsun truck was going ninety miles an hour and it hit us right in the back.

John: Oh my god.

Anne: You can guess what I felt like. I thought it was some little old animal or something, and it was ... it was a drunk soldier in the Datsun truck. [*laughs*]

John: Ninety miles an hour? Was he hurt?

Anne: [*laughs*] No. He wanted to know where he was; he was drunk. He wasn't even hurt. Well, I found out that he was on his way to Fort Bliss – anyway, that's what he said – and along came the Texas Rangers. I mean really . . .

John: Oh yeah.

Anne: . . . you know. They call them Texas Rangers down there – they're not just sort of State Police – and he was wearing like a twenty-gallon hat and he had his guns out and he was wearing cowboy boots . . . I thought that was the end [*laughs*], the end of my life. Anyway . . .

John: Scared you, did he?

Anne: He really did. Anyway, as I was saying, like . . . he, he checked us out, and . . . he wanted to know if there was any damage on the van, and I said we just got some water sprayed on us from the radiator, from the squished truck that had hit us, and to make a long story short, he just let us go. He said he'd drive the soldier into town, you know, and he wouldn't even book him. He said the soldier had suffered enough, losing his truck.

John: Well, imagine that.

Anne: Yeah, it was really nice.

14.2 *Presentation: narrative techniques*

We often want to tell people stories in the form of long narratives. It may be the story of a movie or a book, for example, or a true story of events that have happened to us – or even a joke or a funny story.

To keep the narrative going, we need various "narrative techniques" to give variety and interest to the story. One useful narrative technique is to create suspense by making the listener wait for important information. So, instead of saying:

He fell into the river.

You can say:

What happened to him was that he fell into the river.

And instead of saying:

He opened the letter.

You can say:

What he did was open the letter.

or even:

What happened was that he opened the letter.

Another narrative technique is to involve the listener in the story by asking the listener to guess what happened next or how someone in the story felt.

You can guess what he felt like.
What do you think he did?
And then do you know what he did?
You'll never guess what happened next.
Imagine my surprise when he . . .

Narrative techniques like these will help to make a story more dramatic. Think of more examples and decide with your teacher when you could use them in telling a simple story everyone knows.

14.3 *Exercise*

Look at the comic strip and decide together how you would tell the story using the structures presented in 14.2.

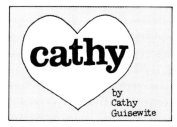

14.4   Communication activity

Work in pairs. Each of you will get a comic strip to put into your own words. One of you should look at activity 135 while the other one looks at activity 85.

14.5   Exercise

Make a secret note of the titles of two movies you have seen – one really good and the other really bad – and two TV shows you have seen – one bad and one good.
Then tell the other students in the group the story of each. See if they can guess the title when you have finished.

14.6   Presentation: handling dialogue

In a narrative we can choose whether to report things people said like this:

He told me to leave.

or like this:

He said, "If you don't get out of here this minute, I'll call the police."

The first way is good if you only want to report the main idea of what was said. The second way is good if you want to report exactly what was said.

Here are some other ways of reporting the main idea of what was said:

He wanted to know ...
He wondered ...
He tried to find out ...
He went on to say that ...
I found out that ...

Decide with your teacher how you would continue these opening phrases. Think of several examples.

14.7   Communication activity

Work in pairs. Each of you will get a story to put into dialogue form. One of you should look at activity 46 while the other one looks at activity 111. In this activity you will have to do some writing, so make sure you have some paper.

We can signal the beginning of a spoken personal narrative like this:

Did I ever tell you about the time I ... ?
That reminds me of the time I ...
Funny you should mention that, because something
   similar happened to me once ...

A story often has changes of direction and digressions. We can signal the end of a digression like this:

Anyway, ...
As I was saying, ...
To get back to the story, ...

And we can speed up the end of a story by cutting out irrelevant details and saying:

To make a long story short ...
Anyway, what happened in the end was this: ...

Decide with your teacher how you would use these expressions if, for example, you were telling the story in the comic strip earlier in this unit.

14.9   *Communication activity*

Work in pairs. Each of you will get a story to retell in your own words. One of you should look at activity 140 while the other one looks at activity 149.

14.10   *Exercise*

Work in small groups. Help each other to remember:

an unforgettable evening
an embarrassing experience
a frightening experience
an experience that made you laugh
a dream you remember
a joke or funny story

Listen to each other's narratives, but don't interrupt except to find out more details.

14.11   *Consolidation exercise*

Sit in a circle. Every other student is called A, and those in between are called B. If you are A, tell the person on your right a story: an experience, a joke, or a funny story.

If you are B, listen to the story from the person on your left, and then tell this story to the person on your right. From now on, everyone listens to the person on the left and tells this story to the person on the right, until each story comes back to the person who first told it.

Was the story you told recognizable when it got back to you? Tell the others how it changed.

Now it is B's turn to tell a story to the person on his or her left, which will circulate in the opposite direction.

14.12   *Written work*

1 Write a letter to a friend, describing one of the experiences you talked about during this unit. Tell the story as if it had happened quite recently.

2 Look at these newspaper headlines. First, discuss with your teacher what sort of story would have followed each headline:

POLICE CHIEF SENT TO PRISON
ORDEAL OF HIJACK HOSTAGES
VACATION RUINED FOR TOURISTS
MAYOR ON DRINKING CHARGE
50 GIRLS GET SICK IN DORM
FIREMEN STARTED FIRES
"GHOST" SEEN IN THEATER

Choose one or two and write *both* the newspaper report that followed the headline *and* a personal report by one of the participants. Discuss with your teacher how the *style* of each report would be different – perhaps look at an English-language newspaper first.

15 *Dealing with moods and feelings: anger, sadness, indifference. Saying goodbye*

| 15.1 | *Conversation* |

Mary: Hi honey, how was your day?
Bob: Oh Mary, it's just been one of those days ...
Mary: Wha ...
Bob: ... terrible.
Mary: What's the matter honey?
Bob: Ah, everybody at the office is sick, the work keeps piling up, uh ... I'm getting blamed for it.
Mary: Oh, well come on, it can't be as bad as all that.
Bob: Well, it is, yeah. I, I can't take much more of it. I, I mean it keeps getting worse. I've got to do something about it.
Mary: Oh. Well, maybe there's another way to look at it, like ... look at it this way. If you hired a temporary typist, now wouldn't that take some of the pressure off you?
Bob: Yeah ... we-we-well, oh, what's, what's the point of hiring a t-, a temporary typist? The typist we got already should be able to handle ... no, it's other problems. The typing's not the problem.

Mary: Well, when we talked about this last week you thought a typist might help.
Bob: Ahh, well that was last week. Now, I . . . I don't know, I couldn't care less.
Mary: Oh honey. Hey look. Guess what I made you for supper.
Bob: Mm. What is it?
Mary: Roast rack of lamb. How about that?
Bob: Mmm. You're a sweetheart. Are you trying to distract me?
Mary: Yes, I'm trying to distract you. Now why don't you sit right down here, and I'll go get dinner and put it on the table.
Bob: Oh OK. You think all I think about's my stomach.
Mary: That's right.
Bob: Mm-hm.
 (*crash*)
Mary: Oh damn it, now that's just what I needed!
Bob: Mary, what happened? wha- . . . take it easy.
Mary: Oh! I spilled the salad all over the floor.
Bob: Oh. Mary, uh . . . don't worry about it. Look . . . it's OK. Um . . . you know, I . . .
Mary: It isn't OK!
Bob: Well, yeah, I know you went to a lot of trouble but I, I didn't really want salad anyway. Um, uh . . .
Mary: Are you sure?
Bob: Yeah, yeah, I mean, well just sit down. You know, relax. Uh . . . it's OK. Look we could still, uh, have a pleasant evening at home or something, you know. OK? Don't worry about it.
Mary: OK.

15.2   *Presentation: anger*

When things go wrong, it's easy to lose your temper and get mad. You may just be annoyed (that is, a little bit angry), or really angry, or absolutely furious.
Phrases like the following express annoyance:

What a nuisance!
That's typical!
That's just *what I needed!*
Good grief!

© 1958 United Feature Syndicate, Inc.

When people get really angry, they sometimes use swear words like these:

Damn!
Hell!
(You should avoid swearing and using dirty words because they upset a lot of people.)

And if people are absolutely furious, they are more likely to lose their temper completely and say:

I've had just about enough of ...
What a stupid idiot!
Why the hell don't they ...
It makes me sick the way they ...
It makes my blood boil when this sort of thing happens!

One way to deal with people who are angry is to try to calm them down by saying:

Take it easy!
Don't you think you're overreacting a bit?
There's no reason to get so upset.
It's not as bad as all that.
I'm sorry to hear that.

Decide with your teacher how you would deal with different people's anger in some different situations. What would you say if they were angry with *you*? (Think of the last time someone was angry with you.)

15.3 *Exercise*

Make a list of some of the things that have happened to you that really made you angry.
Imagine they all happened *today*. Tell everyone about them angrily and let the others try to calm you down.

15.4 *Communication activity*

Work in pairs. In each situation, one of you will be angry and your partner will have to calm you down. One of you should look at activity 115 while the other one looks at activity 42.

15.5 *Presentation: sadness*

We cannot always be bright and happy – sometimes we have moods of depression or sadness. Here are some ways of talking about how we feel:

Oh god! I just don't know what to do ...
I can't take much more of this ...
And if that wasn't enough ...
It's just been one of those days ...

© 1958, 1965 United Feature Syndicate, Inc.

To help us out of our depression, we may need a sympathetic ear – someone who listens and cheers us up. Here are some ways of cheering people up:

Come on! It can't be as bad as all that . . .
Try and look on the bright side . . .
Cheer up!
Hey look, why don't we . . .
Don't let it get to you.

But it will probably make things worse if you say:

Snap out of it!
Pull yourself together!

15.6 *Communication activity*

Work in pairs. One person will be unhappy and the other will try to be sympathetic. One of you should look at activity 103 while the other one looks at activity 59.

15.7 *Communication activity*

Work in pairs. One person will be happy and the other will be sad about some different things that have happened. One of you should look at activity 121 while the other one looks at activity 49.

15.8 *Presentation: indifference*

People use expressions like the following to show that they don't care one way or the other about something.

When they don't care whether something is done or not:

I don't care what you do.
Suit yourself.
Do what you like.
I couldn't care less.

When they don't care what happened or what will happen:

Big deal!
So what else is new?
It doesn't matter to me.

When they don't care about an activity:

What a bore.
What's the point?
The whole thing bores me to death.

When people tell you they don't care about something, you may get annoyed. But it won't help if you react like this:

You're a pain in the neck!
Don't be so grumpy!

The best way to make someone take an interest in something is probably to point out the advantages of the idea or to interest them in a different idea. You can say things like this:

Aw, come on, it's really interesting.
I'm surprised you feel that way about it.
Look at it this way: . . .
I see what you mean, but you know . . .
It's not all that bad . . .

Decide with your teacher what you would say to get somebody interested in some different plans.

15.9 *Communication activity*

Work in pairs. Each of you will pretend not to care about the other's plans. One of you should look at activity 153 while the other one looks at activity 55.

15.10 *Consolidation exercise: moods and feelings*

Divide the class into four groups. Each group is in a different mood.

Group A: You are all feeling angry.
Group B: You are all depressed.
Group C: You are all bored and don't care about anything.
Group D: You are all in a good mood.

When each group has established its mood by talking together, everyone should get up and go around talking to people in the other groups. Try to make the people you meet share your mood!

At the end, tell everyone what you did and how successful you were. Did anyone manage to change your mood?

15.11 *Presentation: saying goodbye* 🔲

Well, the time has come for us to say goodbye . . .
If you're hoping to meet someone again soon, it's enough to say:

Bye for now!
See you!
See you next week!
Have a good weekend!

But if it's goodbye for a long time, or for ever, you are more likely to say:

I've come to say goodbye.
Thanks for everything!

You may want to stay in touch with each other;

Keep in touch!
Don't forget to give me a ring!
Remember to drop me a line!
If you're ever in . . . , come and see me – you've got my address.

And finally you may say:

I'm really going to miss you.
It's been really nice knowing you.
All the best.
Good luck with your . . .
I hope everything goes well.
Take care!

15.12   *Exercise*

Stand up and go around the class saying goodbye to everyone in the
room, including your teacher. Imagine you're not going to see any of them
again for a long time – maybe never again.

15.13   *Communication activity*

Look at activity 45 before you finish this unit.

15.14   *Written work*

Since this is the last unit, you probably don't feel like writing a lot. So here
is just one suggestion:

Write a short report on what you have learned from this book. What seem
to be its strong and weak points?

Communication activities

In this part of the activity you are playing the role of stranger. Remain
seated – some people will come to you for help with their problems.
Here is some information about your role, which may influence whether
you agree to or refuse their requests. Remember that if you refuse, you have
to be *polite* and give a good reason for refusing.

1 Your pen doesn't work very well.
2 You are in a part of town you don't know.
3 Your watch is unreliable – sometimes it's fast, sometimes it's slow.
4 You enjoy explaining words to English learners.
5 Your doctor told you not to lift heavy weights.
6 You've just opened the window.
7 Your mother likes chocolates.
8 You don't smoke.

Someone will tell you what to do when you have finished.

Your friend has taken over the organization of a picnic in the country for
your class. Your friend is now going to give everyone jobs to do. You
don't mind your friend organizing it but you think the party shouldn't be too
elaborate. On the other hand, you realize that your friend can't do
everything alone, so you should try to help in some way.

When you have finished, discuss the differences between the three parts of
this activity.

3

Your group is planning to sail around the world on a yacht. You need to be
as well-equipped as possible without spending too much money.

Prepare a report to the rest of the class to tell them what equipment, clothes,
etc., you are going to take. If you disagree about an item, report it as a
possible or probable item for inclusion. Give reasons why you need or don't
need each item.

You are definitely going on this voyage, by the way – so don't spend
time deciding if it's a good idea to go or not!

√   = Yes, definitely
√? = Yes, probably
?? = Perhaps
×? = No, probably not
× = No, definitely not

4

You cut the following ad out of a catalog because the product seems to be really good and the price seems to be very reasonable. Persuade your partners to spend their money on it.

Save $10 AM/FM temperature digital clock radio 49⁹⁷

100% solid-state radio... a versatile performer! Monitors degrees Celsius or degrees Fahrenheit — install 24' sensor wire outdoors, 6' sensor wire indoors and select desired function. Up to 59 min. of pre-set music; 'snooze' control. Wake up to music or alarm. Earphone jack (earphone not incl.). Polystyrene cabinet; metallic trim. Abt. 11 x 6 x 2³/₄" h. Reg. 59.97.

570 210 662 DL — Guaranteed 1 year — parts and labor. Each 49.97

Take turns talking about your product.

When everyone has had a turn, discuss what you did with the rest of the class.

5

You are student D. Begin by advising A, B, and C how to solve *their* problems. Then tell them your problem:

You are a student and you think you are being kept in the wrong class. The other students are always asking elementary questions and are much less fluent than you are. Of course, you still make mistakes but you want to improve. Unfortunately, you are already in the best class at your level.

Ask your partners for advice.

When your problem has been solved, look at activity 64.

6

You are all customers, and the students in the other group are store-keepers. Go from store to store and complain *politely* about the following:

1 Quartz watch ($49.95) – loses one minute a day.
2 Dry-cleaned pair of pants ($1.75) – dirtier than they were before.
3 Book ($8.25) – two pages near the middle are blank.
4 Two oranges (20¢ each) – rotten in the middle.
5 Bottle of wine ($5.50) – funny taste.
6 Record ($7.99) – a lot of surface noise
7 Briefcase ($32.50) – handle has come loose.
8 Cassette tape ($4.99) – broke the first time you used it.

When all your complaints have been dealt with satisfactorily, look at activity 26.

You are student C.

1 Listen to A's opinion on a topic and say what you think about it. Then listen to B's opinion on another topic and say what you think about that.

2 Persuade your partners to agree with your opinion that:
TOO MUCH GOVERNMENT INTERFERENCE IN PEOPLE'S LIVES IS BAD FOR THE COUNTRY – people get lazy and depend on government help, government programs cost more so taxes go up, freedom of the individual is reduced . . .

3 Listen to A's views on another topic and say what you think. Then listen to B's views on another topic and say what you think about that.

4 Persuade your partners to agree with your opinion that:
COMMERCIALS AND ADS ARE LOTS OF FUN –
magazines and TV programs are improved by humorous, colorful ads, life is made more interesting . . .

When you have finished, discuss the whole activity with the rest of the class.

8 You are an expert on the Wright Brothers, the inventors of the modern airplane. Study the following outline of their lives for a few minutes (while your partners study their inventors).

The Wright Brothers:
Orville (1871–1948)
and
Wilbur (1867–1912)

Orville was born in Ohio, and his brother Wilbur was born in Indiana. Mainly self-educated. Built and designed printing machinery and bicycles. Did experiments on flying in their free time.

From 1899 to 1902, built gliders (planes without engines) to find the principles of controlling movement in the air. Found that they needed three controls: for going right and left, for going up and down, and for stopping the plane from turning upside down.

In 1903 in North Carolina, made first powered and controlled flight. By 1905, made half-hour flights with first practical airplane. Began making planes for U.S. Army and France. Showed their planes in Germany and Italy.

Both brothers were modest, hard-working bachelors interested only in airplanes. Wilbur died in 1912. Orville continued to work with airplanes until 1948.

The idea is to find out as much as possible about four famous people by asking each other questions. Take turns being the one who answers questions.

When you have all finished, discuss what you did with the rest of the class.

9

If you were cut off at home by snowdrifts tonight, how would this affect your plans? Think of something that you couldn't do in that situation.

Discuss this possibility thoroughly. Then look at activity 58.

10

Here is another subject you feel strongly about:
MACHINES SHOULD DO ROUTINE JOBS

Again you have three minutes to prepare your arguments. You believe that it is an insult to ask people to do boring, routine jobs (like cleaning or typing) and that machines should do this kind of work.

Try to make your partners listen to your arguments.

When you have finished, discuss this activity with the rest of the class.

11

Your partner is going to play three different roles while you ask for permission to do various things. Your partner's role and what you should request are listed in order below. Make your requests appropriate to your partner's role and if necessary explain why you want to do them:

1 Ask your boss to let you change your vacation from next week to the week after.
2 Ask your friend if you can borrow his or her dictionary.
3 Ask your teacher to let you go and make a phone call now.
4 Ask your boss again. This time you want to take the Friday off before your vacation begins. Say why that is necessary.
5 Ask your friend again. This time you want to keep the dictionary over the weekend. Say why.
6 Ask your teacher to let you go to the bank immediately. Say why it is so urgent.
7 Now ask your boss to let you change your vacation *back* to next week. Say why.
8 Now ask your friend to let you borrow his or her grammar book as well as the dictionary over the weekend. Say why.
9 Now ask your teacher to let your friend go to the bank *with* you. Say why.

When you have finished, look at activity 84.

12

Your new shoes got wet in the rain and were permanently stained. When you took them back to the store, they refused to accept responsibility and told you it was your own fault.

Tell your friend how angry you are.

Then look at activity 146.

13

You are student A. Your friends, B and C, have agreed to spend the weekend with you. Here are your ideas on what to do:

SATURDAY Spend day at the beach – enjoying sun and relaxing. Take picnic lunch (tell them what food you'll take). Evening: party at Michael's (tell them about Michael's last party, which was really great).

SUNDAY Meet rest of class – take a bus to state capital for the day (tell the others what you can see and do there).
Stay very late – go to a Mexican restaurant (tell the others what they can eat there).

Take turns presenting your plans to each other. Be enthusiastic!
Then decide which plan sounds best, or work out a compromise plan.

When you have finished, report your final plan to the rest of the class.

14

1 Your friend has just come back after borrowing your new car and seems a bit nervous ...

2 Your friend asked you to paint his or her living room. Unfortunately, while you were painting, the can of paint fell and spilled all over the floor. Break the news to your friend gently, because the new carpet is ruined.

When you have finished, look at activity 94.

15

Find out why your friend looks depressed.

When you have cheered up your friend, discuss what you did with the rest of the class.

You are still in group B. This time it's your turn to start short conversations with people in group A. **16**

Try different ways of beginning the conversations. This will build up your confidence for the real goal – starting conversations outside the classroom.

End each conversation after a short time by saying: *Well, I've really enjoyed talking to you, but I'd better get going.*

After a number of conversations, your teacher will tell you to stop. Then there will be time to discuss what you did with the rest of the class.

You are students B and C. You are staying at a hotel. It is six o'clock in the morning and the guest in the next room has just woken you up. He or she is only wearing a towel. Find out what he or she wants, and agree to (or refuse) various requests. Since it's very early in the morning, you're not feeling very helpful or alert. **17**

When you have finished, discuss what you did with the rest of the class. Then student B should look at activity 71 while student C looks at activity 100.

Your friend is late and in a very bad mood. Find out why and try to calm him or her down. **18**

Then look at activity 12.

You are student C. You are very happy to be able to help your friend A get the new apartment ready. Begin by making a list of the things you'd like to do to help. You don't worry about how hard you have to work, and you are free all day and evening. **19**

Wait for A to welcome you to the apartment before you decide together what has to be done and who is going to do what.

When you have finished, discuss the activity with the rest of the class.

20

This is a subject you feel *very* strongly about:
NO INTERFERENCE IN PERSONAL FREEDOM
(for example, the attempt to make smoking illegal in public places).

You have three minutes to think and make notes of the reasons why you think that the individual should have freedom to choose where to smoke, how much to drink, how fast to drive, etc.

Try to convince your partners that you are right – make them listen to your reasons.

When you have finished, discuss your performance with the rest of the class. Try to recall as many phrases as possible that you used to prevent interruptions. Tell the class how successful you thought you were with each technique. Have your partners explain how they felt when you didn't allow them to interrupt. Then look at activity 133.

21

You have several pieces of bad news for your friends. Break each piece of news gently and say how disappointed you are. When your friends tell you their bad news, be sympathetic.

1 You passed the exam, but your friends didn't.
2 Your friends both left the play after the first act because it was boring. You stayed, and the second and third acts were fantastic.
3 You spilled your friends' drinks on the floor.
4 Your car has a flat tire, so you can't get to the party on time.
5 You wanted to go downtown and thought your friends were both busy – you went alone and had a miserable time.
6 You now have to discuss this activity with the rest of the class. Tell your friends.

22

Look at this diary page. It shows what happened to *you* last Friday:

Friday **13** *March*

Morning

FIRST DAY BACK AT OFFICE AFTER VACATION.
BAD START — MISSED TRAIN. HAD TO TAKE CAR.
HARD TO PARK IN TOWN. HALF AN HOUR LATE.

PILES OF WORK — LETTERS TO ANSWER, REPORTS
TO READ, VISITS TO ARRANGE. JANE OFF SICK,
SO THERE WAS NOBODY HELPING. TED DROPPED IN,
HAPPENED TO MENTION GREEN IS LEAVING. ASKED
ABOUT HIS JOB — SEEMS IT WAS ADVERTISED
WHILE I WAS ON VACATION. NOT FAIR! CLOSING
DATE FOR COMPETITION WAS LAST WEEK! CALLED
BROWN TO SEE IF ANYTHING COULD BE DONE — HE SAID
NO CHANCE.

Lunch

LUNCH IN CAFETERIA. TED SUGGESTED CALLING
CHAIRMAN'S SECRETARY ABOUT JOB.
GOOD IDEA!

Afternoon

PHONED HER. SHE SAID INTERVIEWS WERE TODAY —
MOSTLY OUTSIDE APPLICANTS. MORE INTERVIEWS
THIS AFTERNOON. CAN I BE ADDED TO THE LIST?
PROBABLY NOT, BUT PHONE CHAIRMAN. WAITED
A LONG TIME TO GET THROUGH (HE WAS VERY
BUSY). FINALLY MANAGED TO GET HIM.
PERSUADED HIM THAT INSIDE CANDIDATES SHOULD
BE PREFERRED TO OUTSIDERS. GOT THE JOB!

Evening CELEBRATION! GOING HOME, FOOL IN GREEN
CONVERTIBLE PULLED OUT OF PARKING LOT RIGHT
INTO MY CAR. HONKED AT HIM, BUT HE DIDN'T
PAY ANY ATTENTION. ONLY MINOR DAMAGE
TO HIS CAR — DIDN'T STOP TO ARGUE. AT HOME,
REALIZED DAMAGE TO MY CAR WAS WORSE
THAN I THOUGHT — ALMOST $300 WORTH PROBABLY.
WHAT A WAY TO CELEBRATE A NEW JOB!

Begin the activity by asking your partner exactly what happened to *him or her* last Friday. When you have found out everything, your partner will try to find out what happened to you. Don't remember *too* easily – wait to be asked specific questions.

When you have finished, discuss what you did with the rest of the class.

23

Your only pleasure in life is your TV. When you can't sleep you love watching the late movie. You are *slightly* deaf.

When your neighbor knocks, pretend not to hear at first. Then try to satisfy his or her complaint. Then look at activity 48.

24

You have a toothache. And a headache. It's Sunday. It's pouring rain. And your girlfriend (or boyfriend) has left you. You had an argument and you can't get in touch to make up because she (or he) has left town. Tell your friend all about it.

When you feel better, look at activity 139.

25

This time it's your turn to go around meeting different students and asking them to do things. Ask your partner to do the first thing on the following list, and when he or she has agreed, move on to talk to another student. Treat everyone you meet as someone you know, but not as a close friend. Stand up first.

1   You need a good map of the city, but you don't have time to go to the bookstore.
2   You feel like having some coffee, but you don't have time to go and buy it yourself.
3   Your airline flight departure needs to be confirmed, and you know your friend is going to the travel agent.
4   You want to go to a movie, but don't know what times the show starts. Get your friend to phone for you.
5   You are feeling sick and can't get to school. Get your friend to telephone the school and tell them.
6   You are going away for the weekend. Get your friend to call your neighbor to feed your dog.
7   You are busy and can't talk to your friend for two or three minutes. Ask him or her to wait.
8   You have some homework to finish. You can't talk to your friend for fifteen minutes. Ask him or her to come back then.
9   You're on your way to a lecture. You can't talk until afterward. Ask your friend to come back later.
10 Ask your partner to go back to his or her own seat and be ready to discuss this activity with the rest of the class.

Go back to your own seat.

26

Now it's your turn to be storekeepers. Each of you should sit down in a separate place (pretending to be in a store) and wait for a customer to come in. Be polite to each customer and try to be as helpful as possible.

When there are no more customers, you can close your store and discuss your performance with the rest of the class.

27

Now it's your turn to play the part of the accident-prone student. Your host or hostess has been out for the evening, and when he or she gets back you have some bad news to give:

Your dinner was left in the oven, but you forgot about it
    and it burned. That's why there's the smell of smoke
    all over the house.

You helped yourself to a glass of red wine to calm yourself
    down and spilled a whole glass on the new white carpet.
    It was the cat's fault – it jumped on your lap and knocked
    the glass out of your hand.

The telephone rang several times but you never got to it
    in time to answer it.

You didn't remember to pick up their little son, Billy, from
    Mrs. Green's until eleven o'clock. Mrs. Green was angry and
    said she didn't want to take care of him anymore.

When you have finished, discuss what you did with the rest of the class.

28

You have just been fired. You arrived late and were unintentionally rude to your boss. It was a good job. There's no chance of getting such a good job in another company. Tell your friend.

When you feel better, look at activity 68.

29

You cut the following ad out of a catalog because the product seems to be really good and the price seems to be very reasonable. Persuade your partners to spend their money on it.

Introducing

Sears new 8-track music system ... great value

199⁹⁸ stand sold separately

Quality 8-track system

Solid-State AM/FM-FM Stereo Receiver has rotary controls for volume, tone, balance and function select. Lighted dial scale; stereo alert light. Satellite speaker capability. Size about 18 x 14½ x 9″ high.

Built-In 8-Track Player. Push button for program selection. Illuminated channel indicator.

Built-In Record Changer. 3-speed full-size automatic. Ceramic cartridge with dual diamond/sapphire needles. Full dust cover included.

Air-Suspension Type Speaker Enclosures with 5″ full-range speaker in each 8′ lead wire. Brown grille cloth front. Measures about 10¼ x 4½ x 15½″ high. Guaranteed for 1 year—parts and labor included.
570 228 523 DL—System, each 199.98

D System Stand. Walnut Woodgrain melamine-covered sides. Black vinyl-covered shelves. Measures about 24″ wide x 15½″ deep x 24″ high. Assembles easily—instructions included.
570 245 760 DL—Each 39.98

Take turns talking about your product.

When everyone has had a turn, discuss what you did with the rest of the class.

30

You are student B.

1 Listen to A's opinion on a topic and say what you think about it.

2 Persuade your partners to agree with your opinion that:
DEVELOPING NUCLEAR POWER IS ESSENTIAL – oil and gas supplies are running out, nuclear energy is cheap, clean, and plentiful . . .

3 Listen to C's opinion on another topic. Say what you think. Then listen to A's opinion on another topic and say what you think about that.

4 Persuade your partners to agree with your opinion that:
SOFT DRUGS LIKE MARIJUANA SHOULD BE LEGALIZED – cigarettes are more harmful to health, it is legal in several parts of the world . . .

5 Listen and react to C's opinion on another topic.

When you have finished, discuss the whole activity with the rest of the class.

31

Your group is planning a trip by car from Anchorage, Alaska, to Mexico City. You need to be as well-equipped as possible without spending too much money.

Prepare a report to the rest of the class to tell them what equipment, clothes, etc., you are going to take. If you disagree about an item, report it as a possible or probable item for inclusion. Give reasons why you need or don't need each item.

You are definitely going on this trip, by the way – so don't spend any time deciding if it's a good idea to go or not!

√   = Yes, definitely
√? = Yes, probably
?? = Perhaps
×? = No, probably not
× = No, definitely not

32

1 Your friend loaned you his or her car this morning and while you were parking it, you scratched it all along the driver's side. Break the news to your friend gently, because the car was new last month and you promised to be very careful.

2 Your friend has been painting your living room while you were out – you hope he or she has done a good job . . .

When you have finished, look at activity 134.

33

You are student B. Begin by advising A how to solve his or her problem. Then tell your partners your own problem:

You are a student away from home and you are finding life very depressing. You don't think your English is improving and you are home-sick. Your course lasts another six months.

Ask your partners for advice.

When your problem has been solved, advise C and D how to solve their problems.

When all these problems have been solved, look at activity 126.

34

Your neighbor keeps on parking his or her car in front of your house, partly blocking your driveway. This makes it difficult for you to get your car in and out.
Knock on your neighbor's door and complain.

When you are satisfied, look at activity 23.

35

You are in group A. Make sure each member of the group has time to say what he or she thinks. Your committee has been asked to prepare a report on:

YOUR MAIN DIFFICULTIES WITH ENGLISH VOCABULARY

Your discussion should include: the difficulty of remembering new words, how to decide if a new word is one you should learn to *use* or just to recognize, learning to use words appropriately, individual students needing to know different vocabularies, etc.

When you are ready, report your findings to the rest of the class and ask them for *their* comments on your report. Then listen to group B's report and group C's report and comment on them when you are asked to do so.

36

1 Say hello to your friend and find out if he or she is OK.
2 Ask your friend to pay you back the $20 he or she owes you. You need it *today* to buy a textbook for a course.
3 You promised your friend that you would telephone the theater to reserve some tickets last week but it slipped your mind. Now there are no seats left. Break the bad news to your friend gently, because your friend was really looking forward to seeing the play.

When you have finished, look at activity 14.

You feel fine today. It's a sunny day and you're enjoying yourself. Your friend doesn't seem so cheerful, though. Find out what the matter is and be sympathetic.

When you have cheered up your friend, look at activity 24.

You are in group B. Read these instructions carefully.

In this activity a number of people from group A are going to start conversations with you. Let them do all the work of starting each conversation and finding a way of finishing it. Let them ask the questions.
Stand up now!

After a number of conversations, your teacher will tell you to stop and turn to communication activity 16.

Here is another subject you feel strongly about:
AUTOMATION MEANS UNEMPLOYMENT

Again you have three minutes to prepare your arguments. You believe that more machines mean less work for humans and that this will create more unemployment.

Try to make your partners listen to your arguments.

When you have finished, discuss this activity with the rest of the class.

40 You are an expert on the early career of the Beatles. Your partner will ask you questions to find out what you know about it. Treat your partner as an acquaintance, not a close friend.

The Beatles 1956–1964

Richard Starkey (Ringo Starr) Born July 7, 1940.
John Winston Lennon Born October 9, 1940. Died December 8, 1980.
Paul McCartney Born June 18, 1942.
George Harrison Born February 25, 1943.

1956–8 Their early groups were called: the Quarrymen, Wump and the Werbles, the Rainbows, John and the Moondogs.

1959 John, Paul, George, and two others became the Beatles.

1960 They played at the Cavern Club in Liverpool and in Hamburg.

1961 Brian Epstein (manager of a record store) became their manager. He made them cut their hair and wear suits.

1962 Beatles signed up by George Martin of Parlophone Records. He became producer of all their records. Ringo Starr joined the group, replacing the two others who had left.

1963 Five No. 1 songs: "Please Please Me," "From Me to You," "Twist and Shout," "She Loves You," and "I Want to Hold Your Hand." First tours of Britain. Crowds went crazy: start of Beatlemania.

London *Sunday Times* called Beatles: "greatest composers since Beethoven." Prime Minister of England called them: "our best exports."

1964 Success in United States. Tours of North America, Europe, and Australia.
First movie, called *A Hard Day's Night* (director: Richard Lester).

When your partner is satisfied with the answers you have given, look at activity 57.

You are student A. In this part of the activity be *yourself*. The idea is to go around the class meeting the students with badges or labels who are playing roles, and speaking to them appropriately.

You are trying to get each student playing a role to agree to do something (see the following list). Make the requests in the order listed. Remember that your language must be polite enough to be effective, but if you are too polite you may sound sarcastic.

1 You want a cigarette. You left yours at home.
2 You want to know what stamp to put on a postcard to an address in Mexico.
3 You have lost your gloves. You want someone to help you find them.
4 You have to leave the room. You want someone to keep an eye on your things.
5 You've just bought a new battery for your camera. You want someone to help you put it in.
6 You don't understand the word *role*.
7 Your hands are full and you want to turn off the light.
8 Tell someone you have a headache. See if he or she can help you.
9 Ask your partner to go back to his or her seat and look at activity 86 while you sit down and look at activity 123.

Your friend seems very angry this morning. Find out what's the matter and try to calm him or her down.

Then look at activity 130.

You are student A. You begin by telling your partners *your* problem:

You are a student and you are not happy in your class. Although your English is as good as theirs, your classmates often laugh at you when you talk. You have spoken to your teacher about this, but he or she says this is the best class for you.

Ask your partners for advice.

When your problem has been solved, find out B's problem and advise him or her what to do. Then deal with C's and D's problems.

When all these problems have been solved, look at activity 144.

44 You are an expert on Thomas Alva Edison, the inventor of the light bulb. Study the following outline of his life for a few minutes (while your partners study their inventors).

Thomas Alva Edison
1847–1931

Born in Ohio. Educated by his mother and then taught himself. Had a bad relationship with his father. From the age of 12, worked selling snacks on railroad, and later operated telegraph.

Enjoyed being alone – he was partly deaf. Did experiments in his free time and read all the scientific journals he could find.

In 1869, became a freelance inventor. Made electrical vote recorder. Also made stock market recorder (called a "stock ticker"). Made improvements to telephone, record player, movie camera and projector, dictating machine, and even cement-making process.

In 1876, began first industrial research lab (where a team of experts studies projects that promise to make money) and first military research lab. Invented the modern electric light in 1879. Designed electric circuits and machinery to generate electricity. Continued his inventions in huge new lab in New Jersey until the time of his death in 1931.

The idea is to find out as much as possible about four famous people by asking each other questions. Take turns being the one who answers questions.

When you have all finished, discuss what you did with the rest of the class.

Well, it's time for us to say goodbye. Thank you for working through these communication activities. We hope you've found them useful and enjoyable.

45

Goodbye, and good luck with using what you've learned from *Functions of American English*.

Look at the following report of a simple conversation. Work alone and write down in dialogue form the actual words that were spoken. Begin like this:

46

Aunt Mary: Oh dear. It's eight o'clock already. It's time I began to get ready to go . . .

Aunt Mary gave an exclamation of surprise when she saw it was already eight o'clock and said it was time she thought about leaving. She asked John whether he would mind calling a taxi for her, explaining that her train left at nine, and she didn't want to miss it. John reassured his aunt and said that he would drive her to the station – the car was outside the door and it would only take ten minutes. Aunt Mary hesitated at first, but John managed to persuade her that he had nothing else to do that evening, and that it would be no trouble at all. She eventually agreed, so John offered her another cup of coffee, which she gratefully accepted.

When you have finished, give your written dialogue to your partner. Ask him or her to write a report giving the main points of the conversation (without using quotations or looking at this page, of course). Your partner will ask you to do the same with his or her dialogue.

When you have both finished, compare your report with the report your partner started with in activity 111. Discuss the differences.

Your partner is going to ask you to do something. If his or her request is polite enough to persuade you to do it, agree. You can ask *why* he or she wants you to do it, but of course you don't actually carry out the requests.

47

After the first conversation, stand up and wait for your next visitor. Stand in one place during these conversations. Treat everyone you meet as someone you know, but not as a close friend.

Another student will tell you what to do when you have finished.

When you go out, your friend never buys his or her own drinks and always waits until you or someone else offers him or her one. Your friend has enough money. (It's the same with cigarettes.)

48

The time has come to complain politely.

When your conversation is finished, look at activity 112.

49

You're in a good mood today, but your friend looks unhappy. Try to be sympathetic.

When your friend feels better, look at activity 28.

50

This is a subject you feel *very* strongly about:
NO SMOKING IN PUBLIC PLACES

You have three minutes to think and make notes of the reasons why you think it should be *illegal* to smoke in planes, trains, restaurants, bars, movie theaters, and other public places.

Try to convince your partners that you are right – make them listen to your reasons.

When you have finished, discuss your performance with the class. Try to recall as many phrases as possible that you used to prevent interruptions. Tell the class how successful you thought you were with each technique. Have your partners explain how they felt when you didn't allow them to interrupt. Then look at activity 98.

51

You are in group A. In pairs, write down a set of instructions for each of these activities:
1 How to play your favorite indoor game
2 How to make a good cup of coffee

When you are ready, get together with a pair from group B. Explain to them carefully how to do one of these two activities.

Then listen to one of their activities and ask questions. Then explain your second activity before they take their second turn.

When you have finished, discuss the activity with the rest of the class.

52

You are an expert on making tea. Study these instructions before explaining to your partner exactly how to make a perfect pot of tea. Do not look at the instructions while you are explaining.

The British way to make a pot of tea...

Heat the water... in a kettle!

Warm the teapot... empty the hot water.

Tea: one teaspoonful per person... and one for the pot!

Add boiling water (carry the pot over to the kettle).

Allow to sit and steep... for about 3 minutes.

Milk or lemon and sugar to taste. Have a piece of cake with it!

When you have finished, your partner will explain to you how to do something else. Ask questions and get a detailed explanation. Repeat the instructions to your partner to show you have understood fully.

When the activity is finished, discuss what you did with the rest of the class.

53

In this part of the activity, you get up and go from one sitting person to the next. You are trying to find someone to help you with your problems. But it may not be so easy to get people to agree to help, because they are all strangers. Remember that you must use appropriate politeness, and this depends on *who* you ask and *what* you ask them to do.

When you have found someone to help you with the first problem, move on to the second problem on the list.

1 You need a pen.
2 You don't know the way to the bus station.
3 Your watch has stopped.
4 You don't understand the word *appropriate*.
5 Your suitcase is very heavy and you can't lift it by yourself.
6 It's very cold with the window open and you aren't tall enough to reach it yourself.
7 You're in a store looking for a present for your mother. You can't decide what to buy, so you would like some advice.
8 You're dying for a cigarette.
9 Ask your partner to look at activity 108 while you look at activity 150.

54

You have two young children – they cry all night and keep you awake. Your neighbor is just about to knock on your door.

Try to satisfy his or her complaint and then look at activity 65.

55

Try to interest your friend in these plans:

Going to a movie tonight
Helping you do some redecorating at your house
Spending some time studying together
Going to a football game on Saturday
Going out for lunch together tomorrow

When you have succeeded in getting him or her interested, tell your partner to look at activity 147 while you look at activity 122.

56

Your partner is going to ask you for permission to do certain things. In each new conversation you switch to another role. Your partner will make the requests in order, so follow these instructions:

1 You are the boss. Your partner is one of your most dependable workers.
2 You are a friend. You get along well together.
3 You are the teacher. Your partner is a student who often misses lessons.
4 You are the boss again. Ask your employee why he or she didn't tell you that before.
5 You are a friend. You have to write an essay over the weekend.
6 You are the teacher again. This lesson is a very important one.
7 You are the boss again. You are getting tired of your employee's changing his or her mind.
8 You are a friend. Your class has a grammar test on Monday.
9 You are the teacher. You want everyone in the class to be present during this very important lesson.

When you have finished, look at activity 114.

57

This time you want information about the later career of the Beatles from your partner. Get the facts missing from the following information sheet by asking appropriate questions. Treat your partner as an acquaintance, not as a close friend.

The Beatles 1965–1970

1965   Tour of U.S. Made $ . . . . from their concert at Shea Stadium in . . . . Song called " . . . . " was their tenth No. 1 hit in Britain.

Second movie called . . . . made in color (director: . . . .).

1966   World tour, including . . . . John Lennon said: " . . . ." Last live concert was in . . . . Album called " . . . . " released.

1967   Album "Sergeant Pepper's Lonely Hearts Club Band" praised by . . . . and . . . . Song "All you Need Is Love" on TV program seen by . . . . million people. Their manager Brian Epstein . . . .

TV movie *Magical Mystery Tour* described by critics as . . . .

1968   Studied in India with . . . . Album called "The Beatles – White Album" released. Many fans felt . . . .

Made excellent animated movie called . . . . , based on Beatles songs (director: George Dunning).

1969   Disagreements between . . . . and . . . . John married . . . . , Paul married . . . . Album called " . . . . " recorded.

1970   No Beatles turned up at the premiere of their movie . . . . Paul said: "I didn't leave the Beatles. The Beatles have left the Beatles, but no one wants to be the one to say . . . . "

The four Beatles began . . . .

When you are satisfied with the answers you have received, discuss what you found out with the rest of the class.

58

If you became so rich you never had to work again, how would this affect your ambitions for the future?

Discuss this possibility thoroughly. Then discuss the whole activity with the rest of the class.

59

It's been one of those days. Tell your partner about the following things that are really depressing you.

You lost your wallet with all your cash and credit cards.
You have to buy your sister a present right away.
You feel sick after overeating last night.
You missed the bus to work this morning.
You got very wet in the rain because you had to walk.
You have an exam tomorrow and you're going to fail.
You've just had a fight with your girlfriend (or boyfriend).
You are very tired.

When you have finished telling your partner about your troubles and feel happier, look at activity 66.

60

You are all storekeepers. Each of you should sit down in a separate place (pretending to be in a store). A number of customers will come into your store one by one. Be polite to them all and try to be as helpful as possible.

When there are no more customers, you can close your store and look at activity 90.

61

You are student B. During this first part of the activity, you will be playing a role. Get together with the other student Bs and decide who will play which of the following roles. (Have everyone choose different roles if possible.) Then make a badge or label to identify yourself.

I am your BOSS
I am your ASSISTANT
I am a STRANGER YOUR OWN AGE
I am an ELDERLY STRANGER
I am a CHILD YOU KNOW
I am the HOTEL RECEPTIONIST
I am your SCHOOL PRINCIPAL

Now stand up. Different people will come up to you and make various requests. If they are polite enough and their requests are reasonable, agree to do what they ask. You can ask *why* they want you to do something, but of course you don't actually have to carry out the requests.

Another student will tell you what to do when the activity is over.

62

You have several pieces of bad news for your friends. Break each piece
of news gently and say how disappointed you are. When your friends tell you
their bad news, be sympathetic.

1. None of you is allowed out (because you are all sick). Your TV is broken
   and your stereo system is getting fixed.
2. The movie you all wanted to see isn't playing this week.
3. Your friends didn't get the job, but you did.
4. You went to the doctor. He said you and everybody you've been in
   contact with have to be quarantined for a week. You spent last night
   with your friends.
5. You tried phoning your friends to invite them to go downtown with you,
   but you couldn't get through. So you went alone and had a miserable
   time.

63

First listen to your partner's problems and offer to help him or her with
each of them. Then tell your partner your own problems and see if he or
she offers to help you:

1. You have a terrible headache.
2. You have to phone your boss to say you're sick, but you're afraid to do
   it yourself.
3. You're dying for a cigarette.
4. Your watch has stopped.
5. A button has come off your shirt (or blouse) and has to be sewn back on.
6. You feel like having a cup of tea.
7. You've written a letter that has to be typed.
8. You're not sure about the best place to take your date tonight.

When you have finished, discuss what you did with the rest of the class.

64

Begin by helping your partners to solve their problems. Then play this role
yourself:

You are an 18-year-old girl and your boyfriend wants to move to Alaska. He
can get a very good job there, and he enjoys hunting and fishing. He
wants you to go with him, but you aren't sure if it's a good idea. You
know that the climate is very cold and that there isn't much social life there.
Your parents say you're too young to move so far away. What should
you do?

When your partners have solved your problem, discuss what you did with
the rest of the class.

65

Your neighbor's dog barks at you whenever you walk into your garden. Yesterday it chased you down the street, but luckily you escaped. When you complained to your neighbor's son, he laughed at you.

Knock on your neighbor's door and complain.

When you are satisfied, look at activity 116.

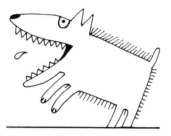

66

This time it's your partner who's depressed. Ask what's wrong and listen sympathetically. Try to cheer your partner up. Perhaps offer some advice or suggest something to take your partner's mind off his or her problems.

When your partner seems happier, discuss what you did with the rest of the class.

67

1 You borrowed $20 from your friend last week and promised to pay it back today. You don't have the money. Break the bad news to your friend *gently*.

2 Remind your friend about the theater tickets he or she promised to reserve for you.

When you have finished, look at activity 32.

68

It's Sunday, your favorite day. It's raining, but there are some good programs on TV. Your friend doesn't look too happy, so find out what the problem is.

When you have cheered up your friend, look at activity 78.

You have just been to a restaurant called the Greenery Restaurant, which **69** your friend recommended. The food was cold, the service was slow, and you were overcharged by $4.00.

Tell your friend how angry you are.

When you have finished, discuss what you did with the rest of the class.

You are student A – you begin. **70**

1 Persuade your partners to agree with your opinion that:
   TOO MANY WOMEN HAVING JOBS IS BAD FOR THE COUNTRY –
   destroys the family, puts out of work men who are supporting families, causes inflation . . .

2 Listen to B's opinion about another topic and say what you think about it. Then listen to C's opinion about another topic.

3 Persuade your partners to agree with your opinion that:
   HOUSEHOLD PETS ARE DISGUSTING –
   people should not be allowed to keep cats and dogs in their houses, they spread diseases . . .

4 Listen to B's views and C's views on two more topics. Say what you think about them.

When you have finished, discuss the whole activity with the rest of the class.

You are student B. You work in an office. You have a very busy day **71** ahead with a meeting this afternoon and you have no time to do these time-consuming jobs yourself:

order stationery: paper clips, thumbtacks, typing paper
buy the *Wall Street Journal* and *Business Week*
get birthday card, flowers, present for wife or husband
put off Mr. Robert's appointment until tomorrow
type minutes of meeting (this will mean working late this evening)
phone chairman to say when you will arrive to see him

Ask your assistant(s) to do these jobs for you.

When you have finished, discuss what you did with the rest of the class, and then look at activity 2.

72   You cut the following ad out of a catalog because the product seems to be really good and the price seems to be very reasonable. Persuade your partners to spend their money on it.

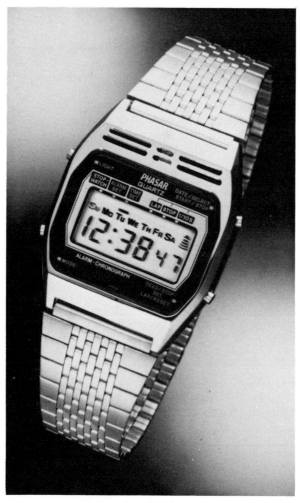

Save $40
Multi-alarm chronograph 89⁹⁹ Stainless

Phasar L.C.D. quartz alarm chronograph with continuous digital readout. Time display shows hr./min./sec. and day of the week with 'A' (A.M.) or 'P' (P.M.). Calendar display shows month, date, day and 'A' (A.M.) or 'P' (P.M.). Calendar automatically adjusts for 28, 30 or 31-day months. Chronograph features event time, time out, lap time and continuous time measurement of two competitors (1st and 2nd place finishes) in minutes, seconds and 1/10 seconds up to 20 minutes; then hours, minutes, seconds up to 12 hours. Alarm display shows alarm set time and on/off indicator. Alarm can be set to sound daily at any desired time, and easily reset for important reminders. Time signal can be set to sound every hour, on the hour. Water-resistant case protects against accidental splashing. Scratch-resistant mineral glass crystal. Has light for reading display in the dark. Tiny battery (incl.) lasts about 2 years normal use. One-year guarantee on module. Adjustable link bracelet.

Stainless Steel Case, Black dial.
040 213 771 — Was 129.99. Each 89.99

Yellow Gold Color top case, Dark Brown dial.
040 213 770 — Was 139.99. Each 99.99

Take turns talking about your product.

When everyone has had a turn, discuss what you did with the rest of the class.

73

You are student B. You are very happy to be able to help your friend A get the new apartment ready. Begin by making a list of the things you'd like to do to help. You don't worry about how hard you have to work, and you are free all day and evening.

Wait for A to welcome you to the apartment before you decide together what has to be done and who is going to do what.

When you have finished, discuss the activity with the rest of the class.

74

This is a subject you feel *very* strongly about:
SMOKING SHOULD BE ILLEGAL

You have three minutes to think and make notes of the reasons why you think that smoking is antisocial, unhealthy, and destructive.

Try to convince your partners that you are right – make them listen to your reasons.

When you have finished, discuss your performance with the class. Try to recall as many phrases as possible that you used to prevent interruptions. Tell the class how successful you thought you were with each technique. Have your partners explain how they felt when you didn't allow them to interrupt. Then look at activity 10.

75

You are in group B. Make sure each member of the group has time to say what he or she thinks. Your committee has been asked to prepare a report on:
YOUR MAIN DIFFICULTIES WITH ENGLISH GRAMMAR

Your discussion should include: particular areas of difficulty, your attitude toward grammatical accuracy, problems of remembering, individual students having different problems, etc.

When you are ready, listen to group A's report and comment on their findings when you are asked to do so. Then give your report to the rest of the class and ask them for *their* comments on it. Then listen to and comment on group C's report when you are asked to do so.

76   Find out why your friend is angry. Try to calm him or her down. (The other day you recommended a restaurant to your friend called the Green Valley Restaurant.)

When you have finished, discuss what you did with the rest of the class.

77   You are student C. Your two friends, A and B, have agreed to spend the weekend with you. Here are your ideas on what to do:

SATURDAY   Get up late, have big breakfast. Go to shopping center (tell them what they can buy) and have a drink in a friendly bar (tell them about the bar). Evening: great dinner in best restaurant in town (tell them about the last time you ate there).

SUNDAY   Morning: play golf (tell them about the course you're going to). Lunch: in Chinese restaurant (tell them about the food you can eat there). Afternoon: visit local museum (tell them about it). Evening: watch TV (tell them about fantastic show that's on).

Take turns presenting your plans to each other. Be enthusiastic!

Then decide which plan sounds best, or work out a compromise plan.

When you have finished, report your final plan to the rest of the class.

78   You have just heard that you failed your exams. You were promised a great job provided that you passed. You can't take the exams again for a year. So you don't have any chance of getting a good job – you'll probably be out of work. Tell your friend.

When you feel better, look at activity 15.

Look at this diary page. It shows what happened to *you* last Friday:

Friday 13 March

Important day! Started off badly: car wouldn't start, couldn't get taxi, had to take bus. Late for interview. Felt hot, sweaty, uncomfortable. Met other candidates— all cool, relaxed, confident. Interview didn't go very well. Selection Committee was aggressive — made me feel aggressive. Didn't make good impression. Asked me to wait outside for decision. Thought of going home but decided to wait anyway. Secretary told me I was still on list of possible candidates. Couldn't believe it. Second interview this afternoon.

Afternoon interview went very well — they asked right questions and I gave right answers. They were just going to offer me the job (I thought) when phone call came in for chairman. Asked me to wait outside. Called me back after quarter of an hour — told me position was filled. Asked why I was disqualified. Told that applicants from inside the organization were preferred to those from outside. Protested, but it was no use.

Evening: went out for a drink. Met George and Bill and some of the old crowd. Everybody really sympathetic. Just leaving parking lot when big red station wagon hit me. Guy took off so fast I couldn't get license number. Over $100 damage. I could have killed the idiot.

Begin the activity by telling your partner what happened to you. Don't give too much information *unless* he or she asks a specific question. When your partner has found out enough, find out exactly what happened to him or her last Friday.

When you have finished, discuss what you did with the rest of the class.

80

You want people to do various things for you. Ask your partner to do the first thing on the following list. When he or she has agreed, stand up and move on to talk to another student. Ask him or her to do the second thing on the list. Then keep circulating around the class, moving from one person to the next, asking each one to do the next thing on the list. Treat everyone you meet as someone you know, but not as a close friend.

1   You want a soft drink, but you don't have any change on you.
2   You want a glass of beer, but you can't get over to the bar.
3   You need a stamp for a domestic letter, but you haven't brought any money with you.
4   You want a copy of the *New York Times*, but you don't have time to go to the corner store and buy one.
5   You don't have time to go to the bank yourself to get some money.
6   You want some theater tickets, but you can't manage to get them yourself.
7   You want to sit down, but someone's books are on the seat.
8   You want to read, but someone is blocking your light.
9   You want your friend to sit next to you, but someone else is sitting there.
10 Ask your original partner to look at activity 25 while you look at activity 110.

81

This time you are playing the part of assistant. Your partner is your boss.

1   You've just gotten back from town. Your boss gave you $50 in small change to take to the bank, but you put it down on the counter of a record store while you were choosing a record and it disappeared. Break the bad news gently, because you were only supposed to go to the bank and come right back.
2   You are annoyed because you have to work late for your boss today. You canceled a dinner date.

When you have finished, report what happened to the rest of the class.

82

You are in group B. In pairs, write down a set of instructions for each of these activities:

1   How to cook one of your favorite dishes
2   How to play your favorite outdoor sport

When you are ready, get together with a pair from group A. Listen to their instructions on how to do one of their activities. Ask them questions as they go along.

Next it's your turn to instruct them how to do one of your two activities. Then they will have their second turn before you explain your second activity.

When you have finished, discuss the activity with the rest of the class.

You are student C. Begin by advising A and B how to solve *their* problems. Then tell your partners your own problem:

You are a student and you seem to be making no progress at all. You can't remember yesterday's lessons and you don't understand half of what your teacher says in class. Your teacher says you are in the right class for your level.

Ask your partners for advice.

When your problem has been solved, advise D how to solve his or her problem.

Then look at activity 106.

Your partner is now going to ask you for permission to do various things. Don't agree too easily to everything! In each new conversation, you switch to another role:

1 You are a friend. It's a little stuffy in this room.
2 You are the boss. You have a rule about personal phone calls on the office phone. Normally you allow short local calls, though.
3 You are a roommate. You are planning to watch the same TV program as your partner.
4 You are a friend. You only want *one* window open.
5 You are the boss. You do not normally allow staff to make long-distance phone calls.
6 You are a roommate. The living room is pretty small and your sister is coming over to watch the program too.
7 You are a friend. You have a cold and think you might be getting the flu.
8 You are the boss. You have just sent a memo around the office forbidding personal phone calls on company phones.
9 You are a roommate. You just found out that the TV set isn't working properly.

When you have finished, discuss what you did with your teacher and the rest of the class.

85

Begin by studying this comic strip. Decide how you can make your narration as interesting as possible. Add detail and dialogue. Imagine what happened before the first scene and after the last scene. You can pretend to be the heroine of the story yourself, or you can give the heroine a name.

First listen to your partner's narration of a different story. Encourage your partner to give you plenty of detail by asking plenty of questions. Then it is your turn to tell the story in your comic strip.

When you have finished, discuss what you did with the rest of the class.

In this part of the activity, you are *yourself* and it's your turn now to go
around making requests. Make the requests in the order listed and make sure
you talk appropriately to the people playing different roles. Remember
that your language must be polite enough to be effective, but if you are too
polite you may sound sarcastic.

1 You want a light for your cigarette.
2 You want to send a letter to England, but you don't know what stamp to
  put on the envelope.
3 You don't understand the word *sarcastic*.
4 You want to change a light bulb, but you need someone to hold the chair
  steady while you climb up.
5 You want a ride home, because you don't have any money for the bus
  or taxi.
6 You want this person to speak more slowly, because you find it hard to
  understand him or her.
7 You can't open the door. It seems to be jammed. You need help.
8 You dropped your pen behind a bookcase. See if someone will help you
  get it.
9 Ask your partner to go back to his or her seat while you go back to yours.
  Discuss what you did with the rest of the class.

You own a house and you have a student staying with you. You have
just returned home after a nice evening out – the student seems nervous. Find
out if he or she:

had a nice time while you were out
remembered to feed the cat
got the bread for tomorrow's breakfast
knows why the front door lock seems stiff

After your conversation, look at activity 27.

On your way here you had an accident on your bicycle. A driver opened his
car door suddenly and knocked you off your bicycle. The bicycle was
damaged and you hurt your foot. Instead of apologizing, the driver accused
you of carelessness and drove off quickly.

Tell your friend how angry you are.

Then look at activity 76.

89

Your best friend had a party last Saturday and didn't invite you. You were upset because you heard about the party from an acquaintance the next day. (And your friend still hasn't paid you back the $10 he or she borrowed last month.)

Bring the matter up politely with your friend.

When your conversation is finished, discuss this activity with the rest of the class.

90

Now it's your turn to be customers.
Go from store to store and complain *politely* about the following:

1 New shirt ($19.99) – stain on the back of the collar.
2 Ball point pen ($1.98) – leaked all over your jacket.
3 Milk (47¢) – sour.
4 Book ($4.98) – supposed to be new, but there are pencil notes inside.
5 Shoes ($29.95) – heel came off.
6 Stereo headphones ($34.50) – buzzing in one ear.
7 Pullover ($21.98) – hole near neck.
8 Alarm clock ($15.50) – not loud enough to wake you up.

When all your complaints have been dealt with satisfactorily, discuss your performance with the rest of the class.

91

Tell your partner about the following problems that you have and see if he or she offers to help you with them. You can decide whether to accept the offer or to refuse it politely:

1 You have a difficult composition to write and don't know how to approach it.
2 You meant to get a newspaper this morning and don't have enough time to get it now.
3 You feel like having a cup of coffee.
4 You're short of money – $10 would be enough.
5 You can't get your car to start.
6 A button has just come off your coat, but you can't find it.
7 You've written a letter that has to be mailed.
8 You have a sore throat and can't stop coughing.

Now listen to your partner's problems and offer to help him or her with each of them.

When you have finished, discuss what you did with the rest of the class.

You are an expert on Henry Ford, the first person to mass-produce cars. Study the following outline of his life for a few minutes (while your partners study their inventors).

Henry Ford
1863–1947

Born and died in Michigan. Attended rural school to age fifteen then got a job making machinery. Repaired watches in his free time. Built a saw-mill on his father's farm.

Became chief engineer of Edison Electric Company. Left in 1899 to start racing-car company. Decided to reduce price of cars by producing large numbers very efficiently.

In 1908, built the Model-T Ford on the first "assembly line" (where each person on the line has a particular job, and the work moves from one person to the next on a moving belt). Began to have parts for cars built in special factories. These parts were put together into cars in assembly plants all over the country.

Was always an interesting character – loved to work with his hands, as well as control his huge company ruthlessly; paid high wages but did not like unions. In charge of Ford Motor Company for forty years.

The idea is to find out as much as possible about four famous people by asking each other questions. Take turns being the one who answers questions.

When you have all finished, discuss what you did with the rest of the class.

93

You are student A. You are staying at a hotel. You have just come out of the bathroom and found that all your money, documents, clothes, and belongings have been stolen. The entire hotel staff seems to be off duty. It is six o'clock in the morning and your plane to Washington leaves at nine – you must be on that plane.

Try to get the guest(s) in the next room to agree to help you. Before you begin, make some notes on the problems you have to solve. For example, you don't have a plane ticket, you are a funny size and the other guests' clothes won't fit you . . . This means that you can't leave your room.

Begin by calling for help.

When you have finished, discuss what you did with the rest of the class, then look at activity 100.

94

This time you are playing the role of boss. Your partner is your assistant.

1 Your assistant seems nervous . . .
2 Your assistant did something stupid yesterday and you lost your temper. Apologize because he or she is a very good assistant and you were in a bad mood yesterday.

When you have finished, look at activity 81.

You and your friend are going on a vacation together. You have been looking through the travel ads and the one shown here has caught your attention. Try to persuade your friend to accept your choice of hotel

Your friend will try to persuade you to accept a different choice. Together you have to make a decision about which place to go to.

Report your decision to the class.

Acapulco
Mexico

Romano Palace

A first class hotel with an excellent location and full range of hotel facilities, from $359.

Location: Romano Palace is located on the Avenida Costera Miguel Aleman, directly across the street from Condesa Beach, ten minutes from the town center and within walking distance of restaurants, discotheques and shops.

Dining and Entertainment: The hotel offers you a choice of two restaurants: the coffee shop "Tres Gracias" serves a buffet breakfast and lunch, and you can enjoy your dinner at the indoor El Establo Steak House. In the evening there is the Quesaria bar for a drink with friends in the main lobby with a marimba band every night. The disco "Flamenco 2000" swings nightly.

Rooms: A balcony overlooking Acapulco Bay is the feature of all rooms at the Romano Palace. Decorated in Roman style, the rooms are equipped with telephone and private shower. Although most rooms are furnished with double beds there are some with king size. All rooms have FM music.

Other Facilities: There is a small shopping arcade in the hotel with a Men's and Ladies' Boutique, Beauty Parlor, Tobacco Shop, Silver Shop and an Arts and Crafts Shop. There are also several parties during the week at the pool with live music.

Sports: Romano Palace has a fresh water swimming pool plus children's pool. Water sports of all kinds are available on the beach.

Excursions/Sightseeing: You won't want to miss the San Diego Fort. It was originally built in the 16th century to ward off pirates, but now it houses a fascinating museum. Glass bottom boats cruise the bay all the time. A cliff diver of La Quebrada taking a breath-taking plunge into the sea is a sight not to be missed. Other possibilities are side trips to either Taxco, an old silver mining town with cobblestone streets and red tile roofs, or Mexico City, the capital of Mexico. Transportation facilities are available.

96

You are an accident-prone student staying with a local family. Your host or hostess has been out for the evening. When he or she gets back, you have some bad news to give:

The TV isn't working anymore. You just turned it on –
    there was a bang and some smoke, so you turned
    it off quickly.

The cat seems to be very upset – it has been meowing all
    evening.

You don't know how it happened, but the lock on the front
    door doesn't seem to work anymore.

After your conversation, look at activity 145.

97

The people in the other group have been getting on your nerves all through this course. The time has come to stop being polite and tactful and to tell them what you really think of them. Decide with the other members of your group exactly what annoys you most about the people in the other group. For example:

They ask boring, irrelevant questions.
They are very intolerant.
They have no sense of humor – they can't take a joke.
They're always asking for extra homework.
They wear their best clothes every day.

Add to this list and invent examples of each criticism.

When you are ready, start criticizing them to their faces!

98

Here is another subject you feel strongly about:
WORKERS NEED LONGER VACATIONS

Again you have three minutes to prepare your arguments. You believe that if workers had longer vacations and shorter hours, more people could be employed, and boring routine jobs would be less unpleasant.

Try to make your partners listen to your arguments.

When you have finished, discuss this activity with the rest of the class.

You are an expert on Alexander Graham Bell, the inventor of the telephone. Study the following outline of his life for a few minutes (while your partners study their inventors).

Alexander Graham Bell
1847–1922

Born in Edinburgh, Scotland. Educated mainly by his family and then taught himself. Became a teacher of music and public speaking, and did experiments on sound in his free time.

Family moved to Ontario, Canada, in 1870. Moved on to Boston in 1872, where he trained teachers to use his father's system for teaching the deaf to speak. Worked on inventions at night with Thomas Watson, a mechanic.

Invented the telephone in 1875. Got a large prize from France in 1880 and started a research lab. Did experiments on sound recording, sonar (sound waves used to find underwater objects). Also studied telephone systems using light beams instead of wires, telegraphy, seaplanes, etc.

Set up summer home and research lab in Nova Scotia, Canada, in 1885. President of the National Geographic Society in 1898, when they began their famous magazine. Died in 1922 in Nova Scotia.

The idea is to find out as much as possible about four famous people by asking each other questions. Take turns being the one who answers questions.

When you have all finished, discuss what you did with the rest of the class.

You are students A and C. You are the personal assistants of B who has called you into his or her office to give you the instructions for the day.

There may be some things that you can't or don't want to do. If you refuse rudely, you may get fired, so be very *polite* if you are refusing. Make sure you know *exactly* what he or she wants you to do before you agree.

When you have finished, discuss the activity with the rest of the class. Then student C looks at activity 132 while student A looks at activity 2. (If there is no student C, then student A should look at activity 132.)

101

You are in group C. Make sure each member of the group has time to say what he or she thinks. Your committee has been asked to prepare a report on:

YOUR MAIN DIFFICULTIES WITH ENGLISH PRONUNCIATION

Your discussion should include: sounds you find difficult, stress and intonation, expressing attitude by your tone of voice, your feelings about a foreign accent, individual students having different problems, etc.

When you are ready, listen to group A's report and group B's report and comment on them when you are asked to do so. Then make your report to the rest of the class and ask them for *their* comments on it.

102

Before you begin, spend a little time preparing your ideas on the topic of MARRIAGE. Here are some ideas to start you thinking:

FOR:
1 Couples are happier when the partners have made a formal commitment to each other.
2 Stable upbringing for children.
3 Parents like their children to get married.

AGAINST:
1 Unreasonable to promise how you will want to spend the rest of your life.
2 Couples are tied together for life by law.
3 Divorce causes unhappiness for all concerned.

When you are ready, listen to what your partner has to say on his or her topic – ask your partner to explain his or her opinions as exactly as possible.

When you have discussed your partner's topic thoroughly, introduce your own topic.

When the activity is finished, discuss what you did with the rest of the class.

103

Your partner seems very depressed. Ask what's wrong and listen sympathetically. Try to cheer your partner up. Perhaps offer some advice or suggest something to take your partner's mind off his or her problems.

When your partner seems happier, look at activity 152.

You are an expert on making yogurt. Study these instructions first:

How to make your own yogurt...

First, listen to your partner, who will explain how to do something. Ask questions and get a detailed explanation. Repeat the instructions to your partner to show you have understood fully.

Then explain to your partner how to make yogurt. Do not look at these instructions while you are explaining.

When the activity is finished, discuss what you did with the rest of the class.

105

You are student A. It's your apartment and while your friends are here you want to get as much done as possible. Begin by making a list of all the things that you think have to be done. Don't forget food – you all have to eat at noon and in the evening, and there won't be time to go out to eat.

When you are ready, welcome your friends to your apartment and decide together what has to be done and who is going to do what. Make sure everyone does an equal share of the work, and remember that it's usually more efficient for one person to do a job alone than to have two or three doing the same job ("too many cooks spoil the broth").

When you have finished, discuss the activity with the rest of the class.

106

Begin by helping A and B to solve their problems.

Then play this role yourself:

You are a millionaire and you get hundreds of letters every day asking you for money. You want to give some of your money to people who can really use it, but how can you decide who needs it most? You just want a clear conscience and a quiet life.

When your problem has been solved, advise D how to solve his or her problem. When the activity is finished, discuss it with the rest of the class.

107

This is a subject you feel *very* strongly about:
THERE SHOULD BE A HIGHER TAX ON CIGARETTES –
because, for example, smokers cost the community so much in working days lost due to illness and in hospital costs.

You have three minutes to think and make notes of the reasons why you think that cigarettes should be more expensive. For example, this would discourage smoking and improve the health of the community.

Try to convince your partners that you are right – make them listen to your reasons.

When you have finished, discuss your performance with the class. Try to recall as many phrases as possible that you used to prevent interruptions. Tell the class how successful you thought you were with each technique. Have your partners explain how they felt when you didn't allow them to interrupt. Then look at activity 39.

Now it's you turn to go around looking for someone to agree to your requests. Remember that you have to be polite. All the people you ask are strangers.

You must get help with the first problem before you move on to the second problem listed.

1 You need a quarter for a phone call, but you only have a dollar.
2 You need to know today's date.
3 Your nose is running and you don't have a handkerchief or kleenex.
4 You don't understand the word *acquaintance*.
5 You've just bought some candy but you can't get the package open.
6 You're lost in a part of town you don't know.
7 You can't read a sign on the other side of the street.
8 You're in a store trying to find a birthday card for a friend. You can't decide which card to buy.
9 It's time for everyone to stop work. When your partner has agreed to stop, you can sit down.

Now discuss the activity with the rest of the class.

Your partner has some information about the early career of the Beatles. Get the facts missing from the following information sheet by asking appropriate questions. Treat your partner as an acquaintance, not as a close friend.

The Beatles 1956–1964

Richard . . . . (Ringo Starr) Born July 7, 1940.
John . . . . Lennon Born . . . . , ... Died . . . . , 1980.
Paul McCartney Born . . . . , ...
George Harrison Born . . . . , ...

1956–8 Their early groups were called: the . . . . , Wump and the Werbles, the Rainbows, John and the . . . .

1959 John, Paul, George, and two others became the Beatles.

1960 They played at the . . . . Club in Liverpool and in . . . .

1961 Brian Epstein (manager of a . . . . store) became their manager. He made them cut their hair and . . . .

1962 Beatles signed up by . . . . of Parlophone Records. He became producer of all their records. . . . . joined the group, replacing the two others who had left.

1963 Five No. 1 songs: "Please Please Me," " . . . . ," " . . . . ," " . . . . ," and "I Want to Hold Your Hand." First tours of Britain. Crowds went crazy: start of . . . .

London *Sunday Times* called Beatles: " . . . ." Prime Minister of England called them: " . . . ."

1964 Success in . . . . Tours of North America, ... , and . . . . First movie, called . . . . (director: Richard Lester).

When you are satisfied with your partner's answers, thank him or her politely and then look at activity 124.

110

This time you stay where you are while different friends ask you to do things. If they ask politely enough to persuade you to do them, agree. You can ask *why* they want you to do something, but of course you don't actually carry out the requests.

After the first request, stand up and wait for your next visitor. Treat everyone you meet as someone you know, but not as a close friend.

Another student will tell you what to do when you have finished.

111

Look at the following report of a simple conversation. Work alone and write down in dialogue form the actual words that were spoken. Begin like this:

Henry: I'm going to visit my mother tomorrow.
Paula: But I've planned to spend the day shopping.

Henry said that he was going to visit his mother the next day, but Paula replied that she had planned to spend the day shopping. Henry suggested that they should travel to town together and spend the morning as each had intended. He asked where he could meet Paula at the end of the morning, and when she didn't answer he wondered if she had heard his question. She assured him that she had heard him but was thinking. When there was still no answer Henry said he would have to go but he would meet Paula by the bus station, and Paula agreed that that was a good idea.

When you have finished, give your written dialogue to your partner. Ask him or her to write a report giving the main points of the conversation (without using quotations or looking at this page, of course). Your partner will ask you to do the same with his or her dialogue.

When both of you have finished, compare your report with the report your partner started with in activity 46. Discuss the differences.

112

Last Saturday afternoon you decided to give a party for your friends the same evening. It was a great success.

Greet the one friend you didn't invite.

When your conversation is finished, discuss this activity with the rest of the class.

You have just had a frightening experience: you wrapped up a watch that wasn't working in its box and took it back to the department store where you bought it. The store detective grabbed you and accused you of shoplifting. The detective was rude and didn't apologize when you explained everything to him. You complained to the manager, but he said you should have kept your receipt. Tell your friend how angry you are.

Then look at activity 88.

You are going to ask your partner for permission to do various things in the following list. Your partner is going to play three different roles, and you have to make your request appropriate to the role your partner is playing. Give reasons if necessary and try not to take *no* for an answer!

1 Ask your friend to let you open the window. It's very stuffy.
2 Ask your boss to let you make a short local phone call to the garage to see if your car is ready. You want to use the office phone.
3 Ask your roommate if one of your friends can come and watch a TV program tonight.
4 Ask your friend to let you open another window. It's still too stuffy.
5 Ask your boss if you can use the office phone again – this time to call your brother in another state.
6 Ask your roommate if *two* of your friends can come and watch TV.
7 Ask your friend to let you open all the windows in the room. You think you are going to faint.
8 Ask your boss if you can use the office phone again. This time you have to make a very urgent personal call to your sister overseas.
9 Ask your roommate if a third friend can now come to watch the TV program tonight.

When you have finished, discuss what you did with your teacher and the rest of the class.

One of your roommates, John, is always listening to opera records on your stereo. Last night the noise woke you up at two in the morning. You hate opera. Also, he never does his share of washing dishes and cleaning. Tell your friend how angry you are with John.

Look at activity 18 next.

You always park your car on the street because you don't have a garage. Your neighbor is a bad driver and always has difficulty driving in and out of his or her garage.
Your neighbor is just about to knock on your door.

Try to satisfy his or her complaint and then look at activity 138.

117 You cut the following ad out of a catalog because the product seems to be really good and the price seems to be very reasonable. Persuade your partners to spend their money on it.

OneStep

New from Polaroid. The world's simplest camera.

The simplest camera you ever used. Press the button, and the picture's in your hand! You never focus, never set anything. Just aim and shoot.

Motor drive. The pictures are ejected automatically, the film advances automatically. You can shoot every 2 seconds! Nothing to pull or peel, nothing to crank or wind.

Beautiful SX-70 pictures develop in minutes while you watch—and Polaroid's sharp, clear SX-70 color lasts. There's fresh power when you load. The battery's built into the film pack. And you can't waste film or flash. This camera will not fire when either is used up.

Only 14½ ounces. Fits in the palm of your hand. Long shots, shots as close as 4 feet, flash—just press the button and that's it!

$39 95!

© 1977 Polaroid Corporation "Polaroid" "SX 70" and "OneStep"

POLAROID LAND CAMERA

Just press one button—that's it! The motor hands you the picture. You don't focus or set anything.

Take turns talking about your product. When everyone has had a turn, discuss what you did with the rest of the class.

118 Your friend seems to be in a very bad mood. Find out what's the matter and try to calm him or her down.

Then look at activity 113.

119

You are student B. Your two friends, A and C, have agreed to spend the weekend with you. Here are your ideas on what to do:

SATURDAY: Get up early. Drive to state park. Have a picnic. Evening: return to town in time to see a movie (tell them about really good movie that's playing).

SUNDAY: Morning: go and visit your teacher (tell them about the coffee and pie you had last time you went to his or her house). Spend afternoon in the kitchen preparing fantastic meal for the evening (tell them the dishes you have in mind). Evening: invite friends for dinner you've prepared.

Take turns presenting your plans to each other. Be enthusiastic!
Then decide which plan sounds best, or work out a compromise plan.

When you have finished, report your final plan to the rest of the class.

120

This time you are playing the role of boss. Your partner is your assistant.

1 Your assistant has just come back very late from the bank (he or she took $50 in change there for you). Find out why your assistant spent so long on such a short errand.

2 You asked your assistant to work late today to finish an urgent report. Now, at six o'clock, you find out that the report isn't needed right away after all. (You know he or she had to cancel a date to stay and work.)

When you have finished, report what happened to the rest of the class.

121

You've just failed your driving test. You've just bought a new car and planned a long trip with some friends. Your companions can't drive. You'll have to cancel the trip, but you need the money your companions were going to give you for the trip to pay for the car. Tell your friend.

When you feel better, look at activity 37.

122

Listen to your friend's ideas and pretend not to care. *All* your friend's plans seem really boring to you. Even talking to other people in the class bores you stiff!

123

Now it's your turn to play a role. Get together with the other student A's, choose a role from this list, and make a badge or label for yourself:

I am your BOSS
I am your ASSISTANT
I am a STRANGER YOUR OWN AGE
I am an ELDERLY STRANGER
I am a CHILD YOU KNOW
I am the HOTEL RECEPTIONIST
I am your SCHOOL PRINCIPAL

Agree to what people ask if they are polite enough and the request seems reasonable. You can ask *why* they want you to do something, but of course you don't actually have to carry out the requests.

Another student will tell you what to do when the activity is over.

124

This time you are an expert on the later career of the Beatles. Your partner will try to find out what you know. Treat your partner as an acquaintance, not as a close friend.

The Beatles 1965–1970

1965 Tour of U.S. Made $304,000 from their concert at Shea Stadium in New York. Song called "We Can Work It Out" was their tenth No. 1 hit in Britain.

Second movie called *Help!* made in color (director: Richard Lester).

1966 World tour, including Japan. John Lennon said: "...the Beatles are now more popular than Christ." Last live concert was in San Francisco. Album called "Revolver" released.

1967 Album "Sergeant Pepper's Lonely Hearts Club Band" praised by critics and fans. Song "All you Need Is Love" on TV program seen by 150 million people. Their manager Brian Epstein committed suicide.

TV movie *Magical Mystery Tour* described by critics as an amateur home movie.

1968 Studied in India with the Maharishi. Album called "The Beatles – White Album" released. Many fans felt disappointed.

Made excellent animated movie called *Yellow Submarine*, based on Beatles songs (director: George Dunning).

1969 Disagreements between John and Paul. John married Yoko Ono, Paul married Linda Eastman. Album called "Abbey Road" recorded.

1970 No Beatles turned up at the premiere of their movie *Let It Be*. Paul said: "I didn't leave the Beatles. The Beatles have left the Beatles, but no one wants to be the one to say the party's over."

The four Beatles began their solo careers.

When your partner is satisfied with the answers you have given, discuss what you did with the rest of the class.

You have been asked to give a talk to all the students in the school about your country. The magazines and brochures you wanted haven't arrived. The talk begins in ten minutes. You haven't prepared it well enough. You can't get out of it now – everyone is depending on you. Tell your friend.

When you feel better, discuss what you did with the rest of the class.

Begin by listening to A's problem. Help him or her to solve it by giving advice. Then play this role yourself:

You are a 30-year-old bachelor and your father has just died. Your mother doesn't want to live on her own – she wants to come and live with you. You have two married sisters, but they both live in Australia and don't want her there. There are no other relatives. You're afraid that if you refuse to take her she will become very sick and upset. The trouble is that you really don't get along very well with her. What should you do?

When your partners have solved your problem, advise C and D how to solve their problems.

When the activity is finished, discuss it with the rest of the class.

Your friend seems to be angry again. He or she seems to have an injured leg. Find out what happened and be sympathetic.

Look at activity 69 when your partner is calmer.

Your neighbor has two young children who are very noisy. They scream and shout even at midnight. Your neighbor doesn't seem to care about their screaming. You have just had a sleepless night as a result.

Go and complain – but *don't* be aggressive! Knock on the door first.

When you're satisfied, look at activity 129.

129

You have a beautiful dog that you love very much. It sometimes barks at strangers, but it would never hurt anyone.

Your neighbor is just about to knock on your door.

Try to satisfy his or her complaint and then look at activity 34.

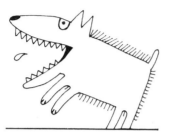

130

You waited for Jane at the bus stop for 30 minutes but she never arrived. By that time you were late and had to take a taxi. Jane is never on time.

Tell your friend how angry you are with Jane.

Look at activity 118 next.

131

The people in the other group have been getting on your nerves all through this course. The time has come to stop being polite and tactful and to tell them what you really think of them. Decide with the other members of your group exactly what annoys you most about the people in the other group. For example:

They always ask stupid questions.
They laugh at silly jokes all the time.
They never do their homework.
Their clothes are always sloppy.
They don't seem to think anything is important.

Add to this list and invent examples of each criticism.

When you are ready, start criticizing them to their faces!

You are planning a large picnic in the country for your class. Your friend(s) are no good at organizing, so you took charge and now you have to tell the others what to do. Here are some of the things that you have to assign to people in the group (including yourself):

TRANSPORTATION: Enough cars for the whole class and maybe some guests.
FOOD: Buy and prepare food, get knives, forks, plates, etc.
DRINKS: Plenty of different drinks to suit all tastes – hot and cold, alcoholic and soft.
ENTERTAINMENT: Music (at least a guitar and cassette player), sports equipment (at least a bat, a softball, and a couple of Frisbees).
INVITATIONS: Contact all guests by phone or personally. Don't forget your teachers!
BAD WEATHER: Alternate plan?
MONEY: Get money from everybody *before* the picnic.

When you have finished, discuss the differences between the *three* parts of this activity.

Here is another subject you feel strongly about:
WORKERS DON'T WORK HARD ENOUGH

Again you have three minutes to prepare your arguments. You believe that if everyone worked harder, productivity would rise and the country would be more prosperous. At the present time workers are much too lazy.

Try to make your partners listen to your arguments.

When you have finished, discuss this activity with the rest of the class.

This time you are playing the role of assistant. Your partner is your boss.

1 You've just made a long distance call without your boss's permission. If you don't tell your boss first, someone else will. Break the news gently, because your boss told you never to use the office phone for private calls.
2 You did something rather stupid yesterday and your boss got angry.

When you have finished, look at activity 120.

135

Begin by studying this comic strip. Decide how you can make your narration as interesting as possible. Add detail and dialogue. Imagine what happened before the first scene and what happened after the last scene. You can pretend to be the hero of the story yourself, or you can give the hero a name.

When you are ready, tell your partner the story. Then listen to your partner's story and ask plenty of questions to get as much detail as possible.

When you have finished, discuss what you did with the rest of the class.

136

You are still in group A. This time it's your turn to be silent until someone speaks to you. Stand up and wait for people from group B to start conversations with you. Let them ask the questions and finish each conversation.

After a number of conversations, your teacher will tell you to stop. Then there will be time for you to discuss what you did with the rest of the class.

When you go out, you usually drink orange juice and maybe smoke one or two cigarettes. You don't see why you should offer everyone else at the bar drinks and give away lots of cigarettes to heavy smokers.

Greet your friend and see what he or she has to say.

When your conversation is finished, look at activity 89.

Your neighbor's TV is always on – all day and all night. This keeps you awake because the volume is always too high.

Go and complain. Your neighbor is *very* deaf, so you will have to shout. Knock on the door first.

When you are satisfied, look at activity 137.

Find out what's the matter with your friend.

When you have cheered up your friend, look at activity 125.

Your partner will begin by telling you a story. Keep interrupting with questions. Later you will have to tell your partner the following story, so read it through now and try to memorize the main points. Then when it's your turn, tell the story from memory and don't just read it aloud.

> One afternoon a big wolf waited in a dark forest for a little girl to come along carrying a basket of food to her grandmother. Eventually a little girl with a basket of food did come along and the wolf found out from her where she was going and disappeared into the forest. After a long walk the little girl arrived at her grandmother's house, opened the door, and saw someone in her grandmother's bed wearing her grandmother's clothes. She soon realized that it was the wolf! Luckily, little girls nowadays are better prepared than they used to be, so she took out her pistol and shot the wolf dead. (*Adapted from a story by James Thurber*)

When you have finished, discuss the activity with the rest of the class.

You and your friend are going on a vacation together. You have been looking through the travel ads and the one shown here has caught your attention. Try to persuade your friend to accept your choice of hotel. Your friend will try to persuade you to accept a different choice. Together you have to make a decision about which place to go to.

Report your decision to the class.

Nassau, Bahamas

Nassau Beach

This first class hotel is one of Nassau's liveliest resorts with action night and day, from $359.

Location: This popular resort is located on beautiful Cable Beach. It is four miles from downtown Nassau and the main shopping area on Bay Street.

Dining and Entertainment: Dining is an enjoyable experience every night with a choice of four gourmet restaurants in the hotel. The Cafe La Ronde features European and American cuisine. For something different try the Beef Cellar where you grill your own steak tableside. The Moana Loa offers a total Polynesian experience with exotic drinks and appetizing dishes from the South Seas. For native dishes you'll enjoy dining in The Drum Beat Club with exciting native shows nightly. For more casual dining the Pineapple Place and the Beachcomber have both indoor and outdoor dining. The Howard Johnson's Coffee Shop offers light meals and snacks. Swinging entertainment nightly (with live music) in the hotel's two lounges, the Out Island Bar and the Rum Keg.

Rooms: These brightly decorated air-conditioned rooms feature private balcony, radio and full size bath with shower. Most rooms have twin beds.

Other Facilities: Shops in the arcade include beauty salon, barber shop, liquor store, newsstand, drug store and women's fashion shop.

Sports: Swim in the large fresh water pool or try parasailing from the hotel beach. Golfing arrangements are easily made at the adjoining Ambassador Beach Golf and Country Club. Three plexiply all weather tennis courts are

available on the property and instruction can be arranged. Other sports available include shuffleboard, water skiing, para-sailing, sailing, wind surfing and skin diving.

Excursions/Sightseeing: There's a wide variety of things for you to do during the day in Nassau. The Seafloor Aquarium gives you a realistic picture of underwater life or you can ride to the top of the Water Tower for a panoramic view of Nassau. Walk through history at Fort Charlotte... or Fort Fincastle. On

Paradise Island you can stop at the Versailles Gardens and Cloisters filled with tropical flowers and historic statues. There are a number of exciting cruises you can take. The Catamaran Cruise aboard the 84 foot Tropic Bird, the Tallship Cruise aboard the 130 foot schooner Keewatin, and the glass bottom boat takes you to the Sea Gardens of the Bahamas. Rent a scooter and lunch on a deserted beach, shop and sightsee or plan an all day outing with your friends. Transportation facilities are available.

Before you begin talking, spend a little time preparing your ideas on the topic of EXAMS. Here are some ideas to start you thinking.

142

FOR:　　I　Needed for diplomas and degrees.
　　　　2　A way to measure ability.
　　　　3　Motivates students to work hard.
AGAINST:　I　Fear of failing exams is unhealthy.
　　　　2　Unfair to students who get nervous.
　　　　3　Written exams don't measure real-life skills.

When you are ready, introduce your topic to your partner and say what you think.

When your topic has been discussed thoroughly, listen to what your partner has to say about his or her topic.

When the activity is finished, discuss what you did with the rest of the class.

143

Your group is planning a hike along the Appalachian Trail from Maine to Georgia. You need to be as well-equipped as possible without spending too much money.

Prepare a report to the rest of the class to tell them what equipment, clothes, etc., you are going to take. If you disagree about an item, report it as a possible or probable item for inclusion. Give reasons why you need or don't need each item.

You are definitely going on this hike, by the way – so don't spend any time deciding if it's a good idea to go or not!

√　 = Yes, definitely
√? = Yes, probably
?? = Perhaps
×? = No, probably not
×　 = No, definitely not

144

Begin by playing this role and asking your partners to give you advice:

You are a 14-year-old girl and your father is very strict. He says you have to be home at nine o'clock in the evening and you are not allowed to go out with boys. He says you can do what you like when you're 18, but not at your age. You feel like leaving home but your mother would be heart-broken if you did. What should you do?

When your partners B, C, and D have solved your problem, advise them how to solve their problems.

When the activity is finished, discuss it with the rest of the class.

145

Now it's your turn to play the role of host or hostess. You have just returned home after a really pleasant evening playing bingo (where you won $100). Find out from your student:

what the funny smell in the house is
if he or she enjoyed the dinner you left in the oven
what message Mrs. Brown left when she phoned
what time he or she picked up your little son, Billy, from Mrs. Green's

When you have finished, discuss what you did with the rest of the class.

146

Your friend seems to be angry. Find out what's wrong and be sympathetic.

Look at activity 127 when your friend is calmer.

147

Try to interest your friend in these ideas:

reading a good book you've just finished
watching TV tonight
going for a test drive in a new car
going for a walk this afternoon
having a discussion about the political situation

When you have succeeded in getting him or her interested, tell your partner it is time for you both to discuss what you did with the rest of the class.

148

You have several pieces of bad news for your friends. Break each piece of news gently and say how disappointed you are. When your friends tell you their bad news, be sympathetic.

1 Your teacher has invited you to dinner, but not your friends.
2 Your car won't start, so you can't give your friends a ride home.
3 You promised to record a TV program about your friend's favorite sport, but it was canceled.
4 You got the last seat on the plane. Your friends couldn't get seats, so they can't go.
5 You tried phoning your friends to invite them to go downtown with you, but you couldn't get through. So you went there alone and had a miserable time.

Read this simple story and try to memorize the main points. When you are ready, tell your partner the story and be prepared for interruptions. Tell the story from memory – *don't* read it aloud!

149

Once there was an old king. He asked all his wise men to summarize all the knowledge in the world into one library of books. When they had done that, he told them to go back and summarize it into one book. Years later they returned with the single book and he told them to summarize it into one chapter. Then one page. Then one paragraph. Then one sentence. By the time this was done there was only one very old wise man still alive. The king told him to summarize the sentence into one word. He spent years on the task and as he was dying, he wrote down the one word and gave it to his servant – and died. The servant brought the piece of paper to the king ... but no one could read the old man's writing!

When you have told your story, listen to your partner's story and keep interrupting with questions.

When you have finished, discuss the activity with the rest of the class.

150

Now it's your turn to play the role of stranger. Remain seated when people come to you with their problems. Then agree or refuse to do what you are asked. Remember that if you refuse, you have to do it *politely* and give a good reason.
Here is some information about your role, which may influence whether you agree or refuse.

1 You have plenty of small change.
2 You're not sure what today's date is.
3 You've just bought a package of kleenex.
4 You don't like to explain words to English learners.
5 You have a sweet tooth.
6 You're good at giving directions
7 You left your glasses at home.
8 You have very good taste.
9 You would like to go on doing this activity.

When you have finished, discuss the activity with the whole class.

151

You are in group A. Read these instructions carefully.

Then get up and start a short conversation with someone in group B. After a short time, end the conversation by saying: *Well, it's been nice talking to you, but I really have to go now.* Then go to another person in group B and have another short conversation. Continue going from person to person until your teacher tells you to stop.
Try different ways of beginning the conversations. This will build up your confidence for the real goal – starting conversations *outside* the classroom.

When the teacher stops you, look at activity 136.

152

It's been one of those days – tell your partner about the following things that are really depressing you:

Your car wouldn't start this morning.
You were late for work.
Your boss was angry.
You have to work late tonight.
You can't go to the theater tonight as planned.
You've just spilled coffee on your lap.
You left all your money at home.
You've got a headache.

When you have finished telling your partner about your troubles and feel happier, discuss what you did with the rest of the class.

153

Listen to your friend's ideas and pretend not to care. *All* your friend's plans seem really boring to you. Even this kind of activity bores you to death!